The Seven A.M. Practice

The Seven A.M. Practice

Stories of Family Life

Roy MacGregor

M&S

For Helen MacGregor and Rose Griffith, the hearts of the family

Canadian Cataloguing in Publication Data

MacGregor, Roy, 1948–
    The seven a.m. practice : stories of family life

ISBN 0-7710-5600-1

1. MacGregor, Roy, 1948 –   – Anecdotes.   2. Parenting – Anecdotes.   3. Family – Anecdotes.   I. Title.

HQ560.M23 1996   646.7´8´0207   C96-931738-7

The publishers acknowledge the support of the Canada Council and the Ontario Arts Council for their publishing program.

The author gratefully acknowledges *The Ottawa Citizen, City Parent* magazine, and the CBC's "Morningside," where most of the stories in this book were originally published or broadcast.

Typesetting by M&S, Toronto

Printed and bound in Canada.

McClelland & Stewart Inc.
The Canadian Publishers
481 University Ave.
Toronto, Ontario
M5G 2E9

1 2 3 4 5   00 99 98 97 96

CONTENTS

INTRODUCTION

Writing about children and families and the staggering silliness of today's parents is something that came about entirely by accident. I was hired at the *Ottawa Citizen* as a general columnist, evolved into a political columnist, and am currently the sports columnist. Nowhere in any of these job descriptions is a mandate to take the stuffing out of "parenting," yet I would be astonished to be told that anything ever written on Brian Mulroney or the GST or the Ottawa Senators ever ended up on anyone's refrigerator door.

The first column, written originally to fill in for a slow day, struck a chord; there were, it seemed, raw nerves out there just waiting to be touched. It was about parents who were doing their children's class projects – including one M.A. who produced a magnificent illustrated essay on Egyptology for his son, who was in Grade 4, and an architect who arranged for her daughter to use a laser for her

Grade-5 science assignment. The response was astonishing. One school board even passed a dictum that, from then on, all such projects had to be done in class, under supervision.

Having stumbled upon such a columnist's gold mine, I naturally worked it for all it was worth. While columns on other subjects might have required extensive research, long interviews, and careful analysis, columns on children and their keepers virtually amounted to room service. Open a conversation, go to a magazine stand, simply stand in a hockey rink or on a baseball diamond or a soccer field and watch for half an hour – and a column was certain to follow.

At the local convenience store, I noticed a magazine called *Dad* one slow morning. *Dad: The Magazine for Today's Involved Father* was a New York-based publication that promised to be "the magazine for you, today's involved father." It carried stories on everything from preparing for the high cost of college to taking children out to fancy restaurants – "When possible, ask that beverages be served in small, flat-bottomed glasses, not stemware." In the premier issue of *Dad*, the magazine that promised to serve as a guide for all the children and problems to come, the main feature article was "Is Vasectomy For You?" There was, appropriately, never a second issue.

In the children's section of the local library, our youngest pulled out an illustrated volume called *Tim Learns about Mutual Funds*. A column on this madness and other library insanity – keener parents who would hoard books, and even rip out pages, to ensure their precious ones had the inside track on assignments – earned such gratitude from beleaguered librarians that when *Tim Learns about Mutual Funds* was finally taken out of circulation earlier this year, they passed it on as a memento, and it remains a most prized possession.

In the local video store, the racks held a short film called *Where Did I Come From?* to help those parents who had learned their sex in the streets make sure their own children didn't have such a callous introduction. According to *Where Did I Come From?*, sex is an encounter between hundreds of smiling little sperm swimming up a pink channel toward a tittering, frilly-dressed egg, the act itself involving synchronized swimming by the excited sperm and classical music as suitable mood enhancer.

How, I ask, could a columnist miss? There was a university in California that offered a course to teach parents how to talk to their unborn child, the presumption being that the baby would be born with a familiarity with the vowels and consonants of its future language, meaning speech – and reading, college, success, would come earlier. Another university in New York was charging parents to teach them how to "play" with their children, the parents hidden behind two-way mirrors while trained experts rolled about on the floor with the infant "students." A fitness expert put out a book advising parents on how to guarantee their precious would turn into an elite athlete:

the first exercise being to take a toothbrush and vigorously rub the triceps and biceps of the newborn child four times a day, fifteen minutes at a time.

The madness began in prenatal classes – men sitting on the floor, wincing through their pelvic tilts, men walking around with bulbous "empathy bellies" to share a sense of pregnancy – and it never seemed to end. Prenatal class had barely ceased when there were all the other classes to book: swimming, ballet, rhythmic gymnastics, tae kwon do, diving, judo, piano, drama, learn-to-skate, hockey as soon as humanly possible. (Mercifully, minor hockey never came up with anything quite as absurd as T-ball, the only game in the world played by grown men using their own children as equipment.)

I never had any idea that what began as ridicule would become a cause, but that is pretty much what happened. While the shared childhood memory of my generation might be of neighbourhood gangs and endless summers, it began to look like the shared memory of this generation of children would be of the backseat of the car as they were hurried from one fun appointment to the next. These children were living a life dictated by a master-calendar in the kitchen that would make the daily schedule of a chief executive officer look like the annual office picnic.

Behind all the laughter was an emptiness. In our own neighbourhood there is a park with three baseball diamonds, two soccer fields, a basketball court, and, in winter, a rink. In a decade I saw only a handful of pickup hockey games, and they were usually organized by a father trying to recapture something lost; I have never, ever, seen anyone play soccer except when it was organized; and scrub baseball is so dead there may no longer be anyone who even remembers how to play it. No wonder in New York they could sell a course on how to "play" with your own children.

Somewhere along the way, we developed a distrust of idle time. Children became an investment; it cost money to join the classes and courses and sports that are supposed to turn them into well-rounded little human beings. It took adult time to drive and wait, and, well, if you have to be there anyway, you may as well get involved. Time is money, money time. And if the child is the investment, what, then, is to be the return on that investment? Certificates, badges, trophies – perhaps even a professional career. There is, simply, no time for play in such a serious undertaking.

And yet the irony is that it is only through play – unsupervised, uncriticized play, where mistakes are allowed to happen – that skill can truly develop. Any child psychologist knows this, but somehow it was never passed on. Wayne Gretzky will tell anyone who asks that he became a brilliant hockey player in his basement and back-yard and driveway, not in any fifty-minute regimen where every drill is laid down and the coach yells at anyone caught out of position or trying something that isn't in the official handbook. So obsessed are most parents – and most coaches, for that matter – with *results* that even these structured practices fall into disfavour, with the preference being for competitive games. Ironically, games are where each child's ice time is, by comparison, severely limited, and where mistakes are not only not tolerated, they are often punished. And then, fifteen years of games later, we wonder whatever became of skill and creativity . . .

Sports are supposed to build character. Personally, I prefer Ken Dryden's observation that, more likely, sports *reveal* character – both in those who play and those who watch. Everyone who has ever been involved in sport at any level has his or her own stories. My own list grows with each passing season: the father who, when our daughter played, offered a dollar-a-goal bribe to a *five*-year-old; the mothers and fathers who have simply lost it, screaming at referees who, if only their helmets were off, are plainly just a year or two older than the children on the ice; the coaches who have doctored the papers so they can get ineligible players into tournaments; the competitive coach who was afraid to cut a youngster for fear the child's father would attack him; the volunteer who put an eleven-year-old up against a wall, skates off the ground, because he had dumped the man's youngster; the coach in Northern Ontario who forced his losing players to ride home in their wet equipment and keep their helmets on for the restaurant stop; the mother in Texas who was willing to commit murder so her daughter would make the cheerleader team; the two fathers in Baltimore who demanded a ten-year-old soccer player pull down her pants to prove she was really a girl.

Each year a new story comes along. When Ken Dryden and I were working on *Home Game*, we were given a letter a Toronto father had sent out to area coaches concerning his son. The letter was in the form of a scouting report, detailing his son's scoring ability and career statistics, his playmaking ability (seriously undermined by inadequate linemates), his character assessment and future prospects. The letter also contained, for the convenience of potential competitive coaches, details of the two teams on which the son played, his sweater number, practice times, and scheduled games for each team, complete with arena addresses. The father who wrote the letter was a doctor. The son was eight years old.

Such behaviour may sometimes feel like a modern epidemic, but it is not a phenomenon known only to the 1990s. As far back as 1940, one American father signed his own son to a formal baseball contract and had the child's mother and sister witness the deal. The nine-year-old had to report for "spring training," had to eat whatever his "manager" (father) put on his plate, and had to promise that he would "follow instructions, advice and orders of the party of the second part, Manager, at all times." The child, G. Gordon Liddy, would find his fame and fortune as a crook, however, not as a ballplayer.

This year, in the Ottawa area, one of the hockey organizations heard an appeal from a father who argued that his young son should be dropped down a level, where he would undoubtedly excel against those who were smaller and less mature. The basis of the man's argument was a doctor's letter, verifying that the child, born in mid-December, was three weeks premature. The official due date had been January 5. For the purposes of hockey, then, the father argued that his child should be considered a January baby, not a December baby, and allowed that extra year of playing at atom level.

It raises an obvious question: Whatever happened to fun? Could it possibly be that we have somehow killed play? A few years back, when U.S. public television was researching what would become the acclaimed series *Childhood*, the producers concluded that the only sensible way to look at Little League baseball was to regard it as work, not play, with its own corporate structure of parents, volunteers, officials, and guidelines. In Canada, the corporation would have been minor hockey, the career line stretching from the first skate to the National Hockey League.

The stereotypes, unfortunately, dominate. But anyone deeply involved with minor hockey, for instance, soon realizes that it is only a tiny, loud minority sending out the wrong signals everyone else tends to seize upon. God knows, minor hockey is far from perfect, but it isn't bad, for the most part. Especially when it's left to the players themselves.

A couple of seasons ago, the team I was coaching began keeping their shinpad tape in a single ball. At the end of the game, they would undress and, instead of the usual throwing of the tape at each other's heads, they would wrap it onto the ever-growing ball that my son, Gordie, kept in his equipment bag. By Christmas, the tape-ball was as big as a turkey, and when one of the young defencemen, Andrew, suddenly had to drop off the team and undergo heart surgery, the team decided to sign the ball and take it to him at the hospital. He kept the silly thing by his bedside through the operation and his recovery. When he came back last season – and believe me, no one plays with more heart – he insisted they start up another tape-ball. A team tradition now.

The author is grateful to *The Ottawa Citizen* publisher Russ Mills, editor Jim Travers, managing editor Sharon Burnside, and the editors he has answered to – Graham Parley, Tom Casey, Doug Fischer – for the opportunities and support of the past decade. Also, thanks to the summer version of CBC's "Morningside" and to *City Parent* magazine. Some of the stories included here appear as first printed or broadcast, some have been adapted, and some material is brand-new.

PROLOGUE
The Seven A.M. Practice

It would never make a highlight film – even the most modern cameras need a *certain* amount of light to work with – but after a decade or more of minor hockey, it is the 7:00 A.M. practice that tends to stick in the brain. Long after the first goal, the tournaments, the championship games, the annual general meetings, and the year-end parties have faded, the memory of that most-dreaded of all practice times remains. There is just something about setting a weekend alarm for 5:40 A.M., something about waking up every thirty minutes to make sure the alarm isn't about to go off, something about the way the kitchen light strikes the eyes like thrown acid while the radio warns of a wind-chill factor that tells you Hell has not only frozen over, they're halfway through the flood – and you'd better get a move on.

For those of us most deeply involved in this strange winter ritual – coaches, assistant coaches, managers, trainers, volunteers, canteen workers, parents – the coming of spring and the end of the 7:00 A.M. practice is a bit like suddenly finding yourself out of work. So used have we become to puck-black weekend mornings, kids screaming and twisting to be left under the covers, missed breakfasts, yelling from the bottom of the stairs, threats from the top of the stairs, buried windshields, cars that barely turn over, squealing heater fans, square tires, unploughed back streets, stalling, stiff steering, going to the wrong rink, forgetting to pick up the goalie, kids that keep nodding off in the backseat, howling parking-lot wind, Zamboni fumes, and bad coffee, that we don't know what to do with ourselves when it is finally over.

Perhaps it is God's little hockey joke, but the minor-hockey season seems to end each year with the arrival of what is called "Daylight Savings Time." The last practice often coincides with the little notice on the front of the morning paper that reminds us all to move our clocks ahead. It is the time, they say, when Canadians *lose* an hour – an hour they will then get back in the fall. But it is, of course, precisely the reverse for those involved in minor hockey. The papers have it backwards. What really comes with the end of the hockey season is "Nighttime Savings Time," and Canadians don't lose an hour, they regain a life.

And yet it is only then that one realizes habit has become addiction. The adjustment is almost impossible, especially for the minor-league coach. There are not only no alarms to set and no kids to wake, but no skates to tighten, no helmets to fix, no water bottles to fill, no goalie pads to do up, no hurried calls from the pay phone to players who have slept in, no lineups to fill out, no serious little talks to have with those players or parents who have kept a stopwatch on ice time, and no useless screaming for order in the dressing room.

I have coached minor hockey since 1980. It began with the son of a dear friend – we split the coaching duties – and carried on with our second daughter and then with our fourth child, the boy, who has played the longest of all of them. Looking back, I can remember what it was like to start out: the dressing room plugged tight with tiny, sleepy bodies, and, beside each one, like a bodyguard, a translator, a protector, the *parent*. It is, on reflection, one of the strangest sights in Canada: the minor-league coach standing by a blackboard, talking about breakout patterns and offsides, the parents all listening intently and nodding, the players, if they're doing anything, nodding off. The parents are there, ostensibly, to tighten skates and make sure vital pieces of uniform such as athletic protector and neck-guard are on, and yet they linger long after the child can do up his or her own skates, long after even the assistant coaches have stopped listening to whatever it is the coach feels compelled to say before the team takes to the ice. Perhaps it is the price they pay. Perhaps it is the price we pay.

Had I known then what I know now, I would never have wasted time worrying about how to get the parents out of the dressing rooms. It happens, naturally, in the first year of pee wee hockey. And it isn't persuasion or confidence or even shame that drives them from the room – but smell. Pee wee is when the hockey glands kick in. And a coach's speech shrinks to the number of words that can be spoken in a single, deeply drawn breath from the corridor.

Pee wee is when everything changes. The quiet dressing room becomes raucous. Fights, tape tosses, ice throwing, rock music from a boom box, put-downs, teasing, screaming, howling laughter – none of these were there when we all started out together. And they grow so fast, if they weren't assigned numbers in the fall, perhaps we wouldn't be able to tell who they were by the spring.

No wonder this is such an awkward, often difficult, time of life for both child and parent. While the youngsters are changing, becoming someone entirely new, we find we miss the children they used to be. It is hardly like death, but it is a bit like a favoured friend or neighbour has moved away. From now on, you will see who you thought they were only once in a while. For a while you will be strangers, and then, with luck, new friends who have just met.

The season ends, you lose an hour, and you gain a life. But it brings a sad feeling of slipping away. The dressing room has grown from awkward silence to such tumultuous noise that a little awkward silence would be welcome. The stench, in pee wee, would level a South Pacific atoll. And yet there is a sweetness there, as well. Just when the coach can finally fill in the game card without looking up a single last name or number, just when the team is its own personality instead of a collection of personalities, just when those who slipped behind are beginning to catch up, the season – and at pee wee, their childhood, their parents' childhood – is over.

Too soon, too soon.

Part One

~

The Canadian Season

It is called, in that small dictionary that is neither English nor American but distinctly Canadian, "the closing up."

It is distinctly Canadian but does not, unfortunately, belong to all Canadians, since it is a price paid only by those lucky enough to know an escape route that leads eventually to a cottage.

The Closing Up ritual may well be the revenge taken by the gods who watch over those who do not own or, as in this particular case, enjoy access to a thin wooden structure on the edge of a lake.

For only angry gods could manage the alterations that take place during the month of September.

All that remains from summer is the address. Everything else has been reversed: there are no welcome breezes in October; the leaves no longer shade but reveal;

relief is now to be found inside rather than out, in fire rather than water.

On an October morning so cold that the black lake steams, an outdoor toilet loses entirely its July charm.

The lack of running water, however, is not totally without redemption, for at least there are no pipes to drain, no diving required to retrieve a plugged intake valve.

Still, it is hardly necessary to enter the lake to know that it has changed dramatically. A log has been lifted at the dam, and the waterline is now so low that docks appear to be pulling back from the shore.

What boats there are on the lake move, for once, with intent: on Friday, directly from the government dock to the island; on Monday, directly from the island back to the government dock. But what is even more remarkable is that all move slowly, teenagers now as rare on the black misted water as the call of the loon.

There are, in fact, no signs of wildlife anywhere. No frogs along the shore, no more snapping turtle grinning up from his usual teasing post below the dock.

But perhaps this is not so bad, for the only boat not moving directly between a distant cottage and the government dock is setting out with three hunters staring off toward the far narrows, where, in the summer, the weeds are thick with perch, and where, in fall, a moose might come to feed.

The canoe comes up from the shore and is chained to a spruce tree, an elegant creature snared for the winter.

The rest of the summer has been loaded into a small shed down by the water: a half-tank of mixed gasoline, a single flipper, three reels that somebody with half a brain should be able to fix.

There are small plugs to remove from the inner tubes and a plastic boat, and it feels silly to stand stomping in the cold while your own stale breath hisses slowly below.

Summer itself has collapsed, and no matter how hard one tries in October, it is not possible to put life back into it.

A cottage is not at all the same out of season. Sightlines have changed, the smell is of smoke and decay, the conversation has fallen from sunsets to shutters.

Those are physical truths, but the real value of an escape to the bush has less to do with Opening Up and Closing Up than it has to do with simply being away.

It matters not whether this is Easter or Thanksgiving, there is still no newspaper dropping in the front door of a true cottage, no television, and not a single mention is made of free trade.

People here discuss the obvious – the shoreline, the baseball scores, the weather – and take their pleasure accordingly. In the parking lot back of the government docks, someone who has been driving shares a ball score with those who have been loading, and it is the equivalent of pitching in to carry the load.

On the final morning of Closing Up, the first sound comes not from the kindling pile, but from a small voice coming from a cool, hollow room at the back.

"It's snowing!"

There are so many ways in which October has less to offer than those hot July days we are already pining for, but July cannot produce a trail of small bare feet that has melted through the first frost on the path.

What is amazing is not that they have walked barefoot, but that the prints show they have lingered, as surprised by the snow as they will be amazed next year, at Opening Up, by the smell of earth coming up through this same spot.

It is not necessary to have been there to appreciate this oddity, but it certainly helps to be Canadian.

~

IT WAS A case of nature answering the call.

It was the end of another tough year in the history of sports – one more discouraging year when as many players wore suits as wore uniforms and the most-telling statistics began with a dollar sign. But finally, mercifully, it was closing down.

A New Year meant new hope.

It had snowed toward the end of this greedy year in professional sports, but the snow that had fallen had melted and hardened in patches. Right up until the end, the water remained open.

But then, on the very last day, a deep, bitter freeze

descended. It fell over the open water and, overnight, four inches of solid, clear glass formed on the creek on the far side of the road.

Glass ice: something that happens only every few years – and is not to be missed.

"The Eskimos," Margaret Atwood once wrote, "had fifty-two names for snow because it was important to them."

That figure has been much debated since she used it, but hockey players may have even more names for ice: new ice, old ice, bad ice, spring ice, choppy, rutted, scab, crystal, soft, hard, open, lake, slough, pond, creek, back-yard, schoolyard, artificial, free . . .

The best, however, is glass ice. It is rare, and comes itself in two varieties. The first is what the Scots called verglas and is a fluke caused by a snowfall followed by rain followed immediately by a deep freeze.

In *The Game of Our Lives*, Peter Gzowski once described the day he and his boyhood friends came across this miracle in a small Ontario town that was then called Galt and is today known as Cambridge: "The snow held again, and off we went, soaring across roads and frozen lawns . . . forty of us, fifty of us, gliding across farmers' fields, inventing new rules for our unending game, allowing for fences in the middle of a rush, or goals that might be half a mile apart. I didn't know if that had anything to do with hockey . . . but I know I'd never been happier."

The second variety is the glass ice that follows a hard, unexpected freeze when there has been no snow.

Someone noticed what had happened this promising New Year's Day when he was out walking the dog. The man and the dog came back and got sticks and skates and neighbourhood kids, and all set out for the walk out of the suburbs, across the road, past the farmhouse and down to the creek, where the rare ice was waiting.

The kids had never seen anything like it. They lay on their stomachs and stared down where the water was still moving over the gravel. A minnow darted, frightened by unexpected shadows.

Had the minnow looked up, it would have seen Canada. It would have seen children racing and sliding and laughing. It would have seen long searches through the bulrushes for raised pucks. It would have heard a country's forgotten rhythm, wooden sticks on a puck.

Here was Long Pond, Nova Scotia, in the early 1800s, McGill in 1875, Queen's versus the Royal Military College in 1886. Here was the frozen pond, the river, the slough, the backyard. The Patricks and their wooden puck off Nun's Island; Maurice Richard on the Rivière-des-Prairies; Walter Gretzky's backyard rink at 42 Varadi Ave., Brantford, Ontario; Bryan Trottier out on the slough in Val Marie, Saskatchewan, with Rowdy playing goal, not a tooth left in the old dog's head.

At one point, where the creek and the glass ice stretched straightest from one twisting corner to the next, we held a hockey game. No corporate boxes, no tickets, no lock-out, no doom, no gloom.

We played for three hours until the kids could think of nothing to do but lie flat on the ice and stare down through the magic that may happen only once more in their childhoods.

"We shouldn't tell anyone," one of them said when we were walking home.

Oh yes we should.

People in this country need to know there is still a game out there, waiting.

~

IT HAPPENS to us all at some point, it seems.

The idea, when it all began, was to get them involved in something worthwhile, something to help develop character – that all-important, so-elusive quality that is not yet, alas, something they can take in school or you can just pick up at the video store.

No, you begin with the best intentions, never for the moment suspecting it is you who will end up most involved, you whose character will come under the most severe testing.

That's right, we're talking coaching here.

No coach ever knows how it happens. You foolishly signed up for "assistant coach" or "manager" or you were stupid enough to answer the phone one night and ended up talking to some guy on the verge of a nervous collapse because he's putting in eighty hours a week in volunteer time and all he gets for his trouble is yelled at and – please, for God's sake – could you not just take over one of the teams because no one else will?

A couple of days later and you're a coach. You have the uniform – baseball cap, baggy sweat pants, clipboard – but you haven't a clue what to do. You don't even know the names of any of the kids but the one punching the front of your baggy sweat pants and blaming you for doing up his or her skates too tightly. The rest of the kids don't even have faces, thanks to the invention of the hockey mask.

But eventually mid-season comes around and no press conference has been called to fire you. You've suckered so many co-coaches and assistant coaches and managers into the same boat by the same method the first guy used on you that, eventually, the average practice has more parents than players on the ice.

You've even taken the course that teaches you nothing and pretends there are such things as break-out patterns for seven-year-olds and, at the end, hands out crests for nothing but attendance that say you are now a certified Level II coach, which means you can now start wearing a suit behind the bench and chewing on ice cubes while you try and figure out what to do with the kid who says he's about to pee his pants and the game isn't half over.

There are tricks to coaching, as all of the greats will tell you, and speaking from years of personal experience with first a daughter and now a son, the following are passed on in the hope of making better coaches of all who accidentally fall into the job:

The 7:00 a.m. Practice: Dress him or her in bed, while still asleep, and then, while carrying completely dressed player out to the car that won't start, whisper in player's ear that a breakfast of raspberry slush, Score bar, and green licorice laces is only a battery boost away.

Pylons: Either steal or buy several. They serve no useful purpose, but parents who have paid out $285 for the year and risen at 5:30 a.m. on a Sunday morning are strangely calmed by their presence.

Parents: Purely luck of the draw. A smart coach prays he'll get good parents in the draft, not good players. Kids will always improve; parents only rarely.

The Whistle: A worthwhile investment. No one listens when you yell. One or two may come when you whistle. It looks good hanging around the neck, and at least the parents, if not the players, are impressed.

Attitude: Shirt collar up, always look serious when passing the opponents' dressing room, close the door on your own team five minutes before the Zamboni is clear of the ice.

Behind Closed Doors: Once the door shuts, you will find yourself facing fourteen extraordinarily attentive parents while fifteen of their children fire pucks in the far corner. The uneven number is because one of the players is yours – and won't be listening either. Make a short speech to the parents about teamwork and using the boards and maybe trying a pass before the year is out.

On the Bench: Try to keep track of the game while breaking up a fistfight over who gets to play centre next shift. Ignore players who want to ask if you'll be taking them to play Virtual Reality at the end-of-year party. Make a note in your clipboard: "Have car battery tested."

Taking Credit: Kids have an uncanny ability to learn games. Say things like "He's really coming along" or "We're going to have to work a little harder on her skating." Parents may get the impression you're helping and get together on a nice wall-plaque for the coach at the end of the year.

Your Own Kid: Trade immediately. Not to another team, but to a parent on your own team. Kids show more respect for coaches they aren't related to.

The Drive Home: You have bought out the canteen. The handshakes and piling-on of the goalie are over and done with. This is what it's all about.

"You know what it says on the scoresheet," you say as you pull out of the arena parking lot.

"What?" the backseat says.

"You got two assists." You do not say there has to be a mistake.

"I did?"

"That's what it says," you say, a deep inner smile spreading. "You like playing?"

"I guess."

You drive on into the ever-pinkening sunrise.

"Dad?" (You wish he would call you "Coach," just once.)

"Yes?"

"What's an assist?"

~

THERE IS something about skating on the Rideau Canal that marvellously unfocusses the mind.

Skating comes to Canadians as patriotism to Americans, as dog-petting to Brits. The ankles flex without instruction, the stride is as natural as the air. There are no boards or turns or floods to worry about here: one simply strikes out and lets the mind float free.

Free to wonder – to wonder, above all else, what it is like not to be among the thousands who glide with such grace, race with such abandon, who swirl and twirl and skate without thinking about anything below the level of a human knee.

Down past Patterson Creek, a man who moved to Montreal from Northern Ireland when he was already in his twenties, already well past the age when learning to skate is like a child learning to talk, is trying his best, while his Canadian-born wife moves gracefully behind, exhorting him to "Skate, don't just glide."

For nearly a quarter of a century now, this man has
been trying to figure out how it is that Canadians seem
able to float across the ice at will, when he has never
overcome the dread of falling that began to haunt him
the moment he first laced on these inhuman appendages.

His wife skates seemingly without thinking, and their
two children fly in impatient circles up ahead of them,
wanting to be close enough in case money is needed but
not close enough for identification. Which suits the man
just fine. "It's all right," he says. "I pretend they're not
there, too."

Down toward the National Arts Centre, another man
moves like one who has just finished pushing a stranded
car down a gentle slope. He moves with effort, and the
concentration in his face is in stark contrast to the
affected distraction worn by the truly capable skaters.

"I had to try it when I got here from Trinidad," he says.
"I rented a pair of skates for five dollars, fell down hard,
and quit. I figured I was just too old to ever learn." But
his two sons soon reached the age where every child in
Canada skates, and they had taken to the Canadian game
as easily as he remembers once taking to cricket back on
the island. He bought his own skates, and now spends
most noon hours on the canal, trying to figure out how
it's done.

It strikes this man as odd that people in Canada these
days invariably moan with envy whenever he tells them
where he is from. He grew up never having seen snow;
saw it once, briefly, in the northern mountains when he

was posted in India; but never saw it actually falling until he came here. The dead of winter, he now thinks, is the best of the Canadian seasons.

Last weekend he made it all the way to Dow's Lake, where a friend photographed him on skates, smiling happily as he cut a fine figure in this strange, cold country.

"They were stills," he says. "So I looked pretty good."

He tried to explain skating in a letter he sent home with the photographs, and imagines that, one day, when the government office he is with posts him back to Trinidad, he will hang his skates in a place of honour, an enviable conversation piece. And he will tell them of the days when the sun was bright and the ice smooth, and how he found the wind to his back coming under the Pretoria Bridge, and how, for a brief moment, he was able to swoop and glide as effortlessly as a bird.

Perhaps he will also tell them of how it feels when the skates finally come off and he is on his way back toward his office.

"It's just like walking in space!"

Contented, he walks up from the National Arts Centre with hundreds of Canadians who have not given a second thought to the wonder of skating since they were too young to remember. Who might find out, as adults, that such thoughts are worth savouring a moment on a weekend like this.

～

I DO NOT know if there is an "aiding and abetting" charge to truancy – but if so, I am guilty and more than willing to do the time.

It was worth it.

Still, it did seem strange to be suggesting to an eleven-year-old that he skip school for the day.

I have, after all, been railing for years against parents who haul their children out of classes so they can tack an extra week on the Christmas recess or March Break and spend it down in Orlando while everyone else is still back home dealing with snow and long division.

I have said it is wrong, probably illegal – and besides, if we can't afford to go to the movies together, how on earth were we ever going to pay for two weeks at DisneyWorld?

But then this happened.

Wayne Gretzky came to town.

To some, that might not mean much – but they do not carry his cards in hard plastic holders. They don't understand what this game can sometimes mean to a Canadian youngster.

That I do understand this phenomenon is probably because of something that happened to me some time in the 1950s, when I was eight or nine years of age. A lumber buyer for a big-city company sent some tickets to a Toronto Maple Leafs game up to a hardwood mill in Algonquin Park, and somehow they ended up in my father's hands.

We drove down – parents petrified by exit ramps and clover leafs – and eventually made it to the home of family friends in suburban Port Credit. My father's friend – far more comfortable with lane changes and traffic lights – took us from there to the city, parked, and walked us to Maple Leaf Gardens.

In an instant, my older brother and sister and I saw more people in a single building than we had seen in total, anywhere, in our lives.

But that is not what we remember: we remember a man in a red sweater with No. 9 on his back, and a father, stiff in a Sunday suit, leaning over to say, "That's Gordie Howe – don't you ever forget you saw him play."

We never have. And never will.

Now, nearly four decades later, I find the same urge to say the same thing to another impressionable youngster, only this time the number to be pointed out is 99 and the name Wayne Gretzky.

We did not have tickets to the actual game he had come to town to play, but because my job these past few years has been to cover NHL hockey games, I am sometimes able to sneak an extra body into the morning practice.

When the youngster left for school that day, he carried a note from home: "Dear Teacher, please excuse Gordie between the hours of 11:00 and 1:00. He has to see Wayne Gretzky."

At least I was being honest. When we got to the rink, there were other parents arriving with other children, and one man sheepishly confessed to sending a note in saying his two youngsters had "appointments" downtown. Not an appointment with doctors or even destiny — but with history.

They had all come to show their children one who, like Gordie Howe, will not pass this way again. "He has his own way of skating," my own truant said at one point during the practice.

Yes. And of passing. And of seeing. And of thinking.

He is almost impossible to describe in words. "Gretzky is like an invisible man," assistant Soviet coach Ivan Dmitriev once said. "He appears out of nowhere, passes to nowhere, and a goal is scored." George Plimpton said he has the ability to "materialize abruptly here and there on the ice." Peter Gzowski called him "quick as a whisper."

That is why he should be seen if at all possible, because only then can you understand what such words mean.

Now, well into his thirties and no longer able to skate as he once did, the whispers are mostly about him. He has all the records, they say, he will know when to retire.

But no matter when it comes, it will feel too soon, both for him and for those who wait around to see him at the end of the morning skate. Perhaps the on-ice skills must dwindle, but off-ice there is still an impressive grace to observe. In a world where other sports heroes spit at the cameras and scream obscenities and brush by the innocent children, this one will still stand outside in the bitter cold and sign thirty, forty, fifty autographs and then apologize when he must finally leave.

Just as Gordie Howe would have done in the 1950s.

The practice took little more than an hour out of the school year, but it will last forever. The father who first drove down from the mill would still ask, well into his eighties, if those lucky children he took to see Gordie Howe still remembered – and of course they did. In the same way, this child who skipped school on a cold January day will have something he can talk about, as well. Forever.

A good teacher would understand.

~

IT IS HARD to believe they could get so excited over a new rink.

In a neighbourhood practically within sight of a brand-new, state-of-the-art, $200-million arena, they have come rushing in after dark with the news we have all been waiting for since that first flake fell, and stayed, way back in November.

"The school rink is open!"

Considering the forecasts, it should have opened a month ago; considering the results of those forecasts – snow higher than anyone has noticed since childhood – it is a wonder it has opened at all, a wonder that anyone could even find a surface on which to begin the flooding.

They are the true Santas of this nation, those good-hearted, bundled-up neighbours who come at night with their shovels and firehoses and leave pure magic for the morning. I did it myself for years and still remember those long evenings under the stars when the air is so cold, the water seems to steam when it leaves the hose.

One day, unfortunately, even the very youngest of those you do this for starts showing more interest in the latest band from Seattle than the current team from Montreal, and the job passes on from one neighbour with teenagers to another neighbour with new skaters. To you, from failing hands, we throw the shovel . . .

This evening, however, the ones we thought we'd lost wish to return to their childhood, and who among us would not want to join them?

With hockey skates and figure skates, sticks, a puck, a dog, thick gloves and hats and unlaced boots, they head out into a night where the city light hangs in the cloud and a light snow comes out of the wind like tiny pins on exposed cheeks.

The boots come off easily and make pads to sit on while bare hands race to lace up skates before the dog runs off with the gloves.

There is continuity here, and far more than a linking of childhood and teenage years. In the nearby city, where the lights shine from, the people once skated so much that around the turn of the last century a British traveller wrote that the people of Ottawa actually walk differently than people in other parts of the world. They have a grace and firmness of step, he told his readers, that "can be acquired in no other way" but by constant skating.

The first rink went up here in 1884. A band played in the afternoons and a season's pass cost two dollars.

Season's tickets to the games being played at the brand-new, state-of-the-art, $200-million arena would amount to a steep mortgage back in 1884.

And yet, there is something magnificent about skating that remains the same. The way hard, natural ice rolls and bumps beneath the blades. The way a young girl can stand like a scarecrow, arms dangling out, and simply let the wind carry her. The way a foot feels like an unnatural limb at the end of a long skate when it returns to the boot and the boots begin the long return home.

It is not only free, it is instructive. The diminishing of puck-handling skills among young Canadian hockey players, you now realize, is directly connected to formal arena practices, where there are no longer dogs around to hound the puck. You also rediscover that hockey will always be a game that is more fun to play than watch.

But it is skating we have come here for, and skating that reminds us that there really are wonders to living in such a country as this, and perhaps none of them quite so exhilarating as the feeling that comes when feet have known since childhood what to do, and how a single stride can begin such a magical ride.

And how strange to do this almost within sight of a brand-new, state-of-the-art, $200-million arena, where parking, tickets, souvenirs, food, and drink now make professional hockey the most expensive game in the world to watch.

We skate on, wondering if we have somehow forgotten how sweetly and innocently this all began.

On nothing more than a sheet of ice. Freshly flooded and waiting.

~

PHIL BOURQUE'S toque will not be going to the Hockey Hall of Fame.

Which is a bit of a shame, really, in that it tells us things about the Great Canadian Game that will never show up in a late score or the official statistics.

Phil Bourque hardly has the numbers for induction: a dozen or so NHL seasons, stints with the Pittsburgh Penguins, New York Rangers, and Ottawa Senators, lots of time in the minors, less than one hundred NHL goals. But he belongs there for something he did at the end of an NHL game between the Rangers and Ottawa, something that no one took special note of and for which there is most assuredly no highlight film available.

Not that it would have mattered much to Phil Bourque if there was. Around midnight, when they run the sports highlights, he was still out there skating. When the recorded game had finished and the other NHL players were all rushing for their cars or the bus, Bourque had showered and changed and dipped back into the equipment bag for his skates and a couple of practice socks.

One stocking he wrapped around his neck for a scarf; the other he pulled over his head for a toque, the taper running down his back like a knitted pony tail; and then he headed out into the dark and bitter cold for the Rideau Canal and a long, leisurely, happy skate, where no one would be keeping track of his hits or chances or shots or plus/minus, where no one but he would even care where he was on the ice or what he was doing.

Two games before, Philadelphia's Rob Ramage had done the same thing, skating back to the same hotel after a morning practice. At thirty-five and on the verge of retirement, Ramage wanted to skate on, to feel that magnificent grace that is the poetry of one game alone.

NHL players believe – and they may well be right – that they are the only professional athletes who will still play the game that is their work for sheer fun. They will do it at the end of practices, they will do it after they retire. They do not imagine baseball players still play. They do not think football linemen go out and push against walls for relaxation.

But hockey players, no matter how high they rise or how old they get, still treasure those moments when it is possible to skate and play and fool around, when it matters to no one but yourself. No coach to question, no crowd to judge.

That, perhaps, is the true beauty of natural ice – anonymity.

What happens on the canal, in a schoolyard, on a backyard rink, is of no consequence. And yet it could hardly matter more. This has been a remarkable winter for natural ice, a two-month stretch when the teeth felt too big for the mouth and the ice was as hard and consistent as steel.

Twice in one week I was fortunate enough to be on natural ice with those who rejoice in, rather than complain about, long cold snaps.

First it was with a group of former NHLers who gathered on a beaver pond for some shinny and talked about what an outdoor ice surface can mean to a young kid trying to learn the Great Canadian Game.

They talked about the lack of time restrictions. No Zamboni to shoo you off. No schedule on the refrigerator door. And they talked about the skills one can only learn here, never in a structured practice or game. Here you must control a puck around players, not pylons, and if you make mistakes, it matters to no one. And if you choose to keep on making mistakes until, finally, what you have in mind works, then the only limits are frozen toes and supper.

A couple of days later, a middle-aged man, a young boy, and two young girls spent two happy hours shovelling a schoolyard rink and then two more playing shinny.

The youngest worked on a "Teemu Selanne move" in which the Finnish star, now with the Mighty Ducks of Anaheim, drops the puck back from his stick to his skates and then kicks it back onto the blade of his stick – a pretty trick perfected on the outdoor rinks around Helsinki.

All afternoon the youngster worked on this move, the puck slipping through, kicking off, going everywhere except where it was supposed to go.

On an indoor rink, he would not have had the time, and others would not have had the patience.

Finally, on a late-afternoon rush, the puck dropped, clicked perfectly, and danced up onto the blade, the youngster screaming "Teemu Selanne!" as the puck slipped around the middle-aged defender and in between the two heavy boots serving as goalposts.

A great play, a child's play, recorded by no one.

But one that would be deeply appreciated by a couple of aging NHLers who chose to bundle up and head out into the bitter cold, when a warm bus was waiting.

~

THOSE OF US who watch too much television at certain times of the year – and who are too poor to afford a hand zapper – invariably discover there are ads that are repeated so endlessly we start praying that whatever series we had been so looking forward to is now over in four straight.

The one that is bothering me at the moment is pushing the Canon video recorder that goes one up on setting great memories in stone.

The ad is nothing if not slick. The family in question can't remember where they went last summer, who they met, or what they did. If these dummies had only had a Canon video recorder, however, they'd have it all on tape for ready reference in the unlikely event some poor relative or neighbour happened to make the mistake of asking where they went last summer or who they met or what they did.

But I'm still not convinced videotape is the proper permanent storage space for memories.

I say this having seen a sweet memory – make that two heavenly memories – strike Earth the other night in a suburban rink where the only witnesses were parents, who never see anything in the right light, and little kids, who see only what they want.

For two seasons now, we have been talking about the inevitable goal that must come to all hockey players who show up for every game and every practice, even at seven o'clock on a Sunday morning.

Finally, it happened, and if Foster Hewitt were still alive, this is how he would have described it: "A scramble in front, a scramble to the side, a scramble in the corner, a scramble along the boards, a scramble to get up, the puck squirts out, a stick hits it! He shoots! He scores!"

In the stands there is only laughter. On the scoreboard there is nothing, the novice convener having mercifully decided that parents don't need statistics quite as much as they think they do.

But on the ice it is as if the five flushed faces have just

won the World Series and the Stanley Cup and the next federal election.

Later, when he is home, the player who scored will describe what happened: the puck was whipping around the ice as the sleek Soviet novice unit moved in, until one of the opponents foolishly committed; a drop pass, a behind-the-back pass, and the superstar one-timed it high off the crossbar . . .

The coach who listens to this story is reminded of another such moment, when the current superstar's older sister was five years old and played in a league where some of the kids took bathroom breaks and others should have. She played one game in goal and happened to stop the other team's single shot with the back of her skate blade, having turned in the net to stare off at the Zamboni.

Now she remembers that game as if it were a Ken Danby painting, her crouched and hanging onto her shutout, her kicking out whatever the mighty opponents could throw at her.

The coach has, thanks to a mother who saved everything, a faded newspaper clip of his own first glorious moment on the ice. The local paper wrote it up as a "spectacular solo rush," though it was, in fact, a goal much like the one scored the other night, and a "spectacular solo rush" would have smashed him into the boards they used to divide the rink in half so two tiny games could go on at once.

It is a shame small-town papers no longer create harmless myths for very small dreamers. And big-town papers would cover the story only if the kid were getting an allowance of $3.2 million over four years and had just checked out of a re-hab centre.

A few minutes after this coach's kid got his first ever goal, another scramble sent the puck in the direction of the other coach's kid, and it happened again.

Or, as the kid later put it: "I ripped it into the far corner."

The coaches could only grin at each other, knowing how fortunate they were not to have it on videotape. Both, after all, still dream themselves each Monday night, when there are not even parents in the stands to watch.

I have seen this man make moves that must, in his head, anyway, be good enough for the sports channel's weekly highlights. I would like to think he has seen the same from me, though it is highly unlikely, as I am a consummate team player who has dedicated his life to backchecking.

But both of us have played old-timer tournaments where the organizers have videotaped the games and then wondered why the teams seem to watch for about two minutes and then move off to order another beer and sit alone, in a far corner, staring into it.

The reason is that Canon is wrong: what happens on tape didn't happen at all.

And the replays that are worth keeping only get better and better as time goes on.

~

"*W*e *stand beneath the pines,*" Catharine Parr Traill wrote a century ago, "*and enter the grand pillared aisles with a feeling of mute reverence.*"

Obviously, Catharine Parr Traill never visited a cut-your-own tree farm in the weeks leading up to Christmas. Had she, she might have been tempted to redraft her thoughts a touch:

"*We scurry among the bent and broken and hideously twisted trees — according to the smiling man at the gate, they are Scotch pine — and, armed with rusted hatchets, we enter the grand aisles to be pilloried, and where later we pray silently for forgiveness, having just handed over twenty-five dollars for the privilege of hauling off someone else's scrub brush.*"

For a decade now, I have hitched on the roof racks, tied on a toboggan, gathered up rope and rusted tools, and driven far out into the country to relive some ancestral instinct that must have been passed down in a sleight of hand.

The memory is of a father reaching for a sharp axe and simply walking off into the woods, the kids squealing and singing and scurrying from one spruce stand to the next until a selection is made and the battle can begin to see who chops and who hauls and who runs on ahead home to brag.

The present, unfortunately, no longer has woods one simply walks off into with an axe. The present will, however, let those who can afford to, pretend.

In the present, it is the adults rather than the kids who

run from stand to stand. They move like frightened foxes, darting from one disappointing shelter to the next, scurrying ever faster in fear that the desperate family two rows over will somehow spy the last worthwhile Christmas tree before they do.

For years, I put it down to bad luck – arriving too late or electing to walk down the wrong row. Panic would set in the moment I detected another adult mounting a charge in our direction, and I would find myself flailing blindly into the first tree the kids pointed toward.

Back home, it would seem as if the angel on top were visiting out of pity. People would stand back and stare in awe, stunned by what could not be covered up in tinsel: strings running like a tangled cat's cradle from the twisted trunk to what appeared to be – but couldn't possibly be! – nails hammered into the living room wall.

Actually, if anyone should know better, I should, for pruning Christmas trees was once a summer job. But very little registers on a fourteen-year-old, and looking back on that time, the mind does not fill with perfect trees but with thoughts of heat and salt tablets and aching wrists.

Somehow, I forgot how difficult it is to produce a perfectly formed Christmas tree, how we were taught to use clippers and machetes, and how to dig for goosenecks and spot troubles to come.

"If you don't cut out all the suckers," the foreman, Alf, used to warn us, "the tree'll never grow right."

But Alf had it wrong. Suckers are the salvation of ruined trees, as the twenty-five dollars I gave the happy man at the gate last year for a gnarled wreck would readily prove.

There have been times over this past decade when I've wondered if the definition of a cut-your-own tree farm isn't a place you go to find trees too ugly for the market. Throw up a sign on the road, maybe add an old-fashioned hayride, and not only is it all right to charge more, the customers will volunteer to do all the work. No doubt there are exceptions, but I guess I haven't been down the right back roads.

This year, for once, I stayed on the main drag, pulled in behind the I.G.A., and had my pick of a hundred sculpted spruce. Cost me twenty-five dollars, the exact price charged to cut and haul a tree that even the garbage collectors were embarrassed by two weeks later.

Not only that, but it took all of five minutes, leaving me with an afternoon free to go off hiking in the woods alone, a chance to feel "mute reverence" far away from any cut-your-own tree farm where the happy man stands by the gate collecting twenty-dollar bills – and where the customers, rusted blades ready, race each other toward green and wooden curiosities that pass for Christmas trees only when compared to what's left.

~

We decided to pass on Martinique these holidays. We didn't go skiing in Vermont, either.

We are, of course, among the *nouveau pauvre*, the suddenly poverty-stricken middle class who used to hold down good jobs and now count themselves lucky if they can only hold onto them.

But we still count ourselves lucky to have something, and it does not mean there was no vacation at all. We went on what may, with luck, turn out to be the annual skating holiday.

If we could offer a brochure, it might go a bit like this:

Go when you want, come home when you want. Pack nothing more than an extra pair of ugly grey socks. Stay in cosy shacks only steps from the rink. Guaranteed access to state-of-art facilities. No deposit required.

For simplicity and variety, there is nothing on earth quite like the skating holiday.

One evening we walked to a neighbourhood rink in such bitter cold even the local dog was sticking to the change room; but two hours of skating round and round, on black, steel-hard ice to the glow of small cheeks, and the sweat was soon rolling down our backs.

One day we drove to a nearby beaver pond where the city had ploughed and flooded each night until the pond became a continuing Ice Capades, room for three or four hockey games at once, room for small children better outfitted on their heads than their feet, and room even for an older man to glide about with his hands clasped behind his back.

And on another day, for a bit of variety, the dog and its walker headed off to a nearby creek just to see how long and far one could walk with the ice bending but not breaking, and to watch the dog's mind at work as it stood over a clear part and stared down through the glass at the flowing water it couldn't bite.

There are no slides of this year's trip, no souvenirs. No one was bored then; no one needs to be bored now.

But it is still worth talking about, for if the uncertainty and taxes have done anything of value it is that the squeeze has put people out in the streets in another way as well, and these streets often lead to forgotten neighbourhood delights.

You simply have to tour the outdoor rinks to see what is happening. Staying home is the travel trend of the moment. Bookings have more than tripled. The industry – if you can call it that – is booming.

At least where it is allowed to take off. In Toronto, where the National Shrine to Sport is a $585-million dome where the taxpayers get to pay for corporations to watch incorporated athletes, City Council recently voted to save a few thousand tax dollars by dropping thirty outdoor rinks. Councillors could not even be swayed by a *Toronto Star* editorial that argued, correctly, that the outdoor rink "is what Canada is all about."

Like most of us, I learned to skate on the neighbourhood rink – in my case the one Mr. Munroe built at the corner of Mary and Lorne streets with a shovel and a garden hose. And I learned how to be a generous, backchecking, team hockey player inside the green boards the small town had put up on the school lot, and which the local policeman had flooded when he wasn't chasing loose dogs.

My own father still talks about the outdoor rink they put up each winter on the Bonnechere River and how one winter, in the midst of a life-and-death battle between the two villages, the referee whistled down play, skated over to the snowbank opposite the spectators, who were huddled against the wind, turned his back to them, calmly relieved himself, and then called a face-off at centre ice.

Those of us who lie awake nights worrying about minor hockey – where teams of ten-year-olds can play 160 scheduled games a year and both parents must work just to finance the tournaments – wonder where the great players of the future will come from now that those without money can no longer afford to play.

The greatest innovators in the game – Richard, Howe, Beliveau, Hull, Mahovlich, Orr, Lafleur, Gretzky, Lemieux – all held certain things in common. All played and learned on outdoor rinks. All came from working-class backgrounds. All but Richard and Lemieux came from small-town or rural backgrounds. All had endless time on their hands as youngsters and had parents who let them deal with it on their own – which meant thousands of hours of free, shinny hockey.

Any hockey coach with any honesty will tell you that

a youngster will learn more from shinny or road hockey or from a tennis ball in the basement than he or she ever could from a pylon or a chalkboard or a booked hour of ice a couple of times a week.

And how very, very sweet it is to see kids back on outdoor rinks because their parents can no longer afford to have them elsewhere.

And still they say the government has no idea what it's doing.

~

THIS IS HOW a true Canadian watches the Stanley Cup playoffs.

We are in the middle of the bush. There is still snow out back of the cottage; out front there are screaming youngsters diving off the dock. A week ago, friends on the lake have said, there was still ice around the shore.

The air is eighty-one degrees – this cottage is stuck in a time-warp that precedes metric – and the water forty-five degrees.

Between the melting snow out back and the shivering children out front, we find the Canadian spring. It lasts about half a day.

The game flickers in a corner. The television is a twelve-inch – again predating metric – black-and-white that came from a garage sale specifically for these moments, but sometimes it hardly seems worth it. The closest CBC station is a million miles away, the reception fades in and out as if one final blast of winter is on its way, and the players all have shadows sticking as close to them as Claude Provost once stuck to Bobby Hull.

The Fox Network should look into this. Two pucks are easier to follow. Three are even better.

Sitting, trying to watch, the all-but-forgotten beauty of the Stanley Cup playoffs comes back to you. It is the voices.

Bob Cole, who does the play-by-play for "Hockey Night in Canada," is as close as we can return to the sheer beauty of the late Danny Gallivan, who was to the spoken word and hockey what Roger Angell is to the written word and baseball.

And Harry Neale is, by any measure of any time, the best colour man the game has known. Sitting between spring and summer, with the picture gone but the sound perfect, the Canadian fan simply sits and laughs at the best wit in the game. Neale calls a vicious slash a "three hander," which is about what you'd expect from the man who once coached the Vancouver Canucks and rued that, "We can't win at home. We can't win on the road. My failure as coach is that I can't think of anywhere else to play."

It is telling that, even on a glorious spring day like this, some of us will do whatever is necessary to keep up. It is this way all over the country. Farmers keep up while they plough. The spring goose hunt is on in the Far North, and there are Crees sitting in blinds with Walkmans tight to their ears.

We have all watched so much, there is almost nothing ever new to learn. This year, like almost every year in memory, the playoffs can be boiled down to goaltending. Different names, same story: Turk Broda, Terry Sawchuk, Jacques Plante, Glenn Hall, Johnny Bower, Ken Dryden, Bernie Parent, Billy Smith, Grant Fuhr, Patrick Roy . . . Even when they lose – Roger Crozier, Ron Hextall, Kirk McLean – the goaltender is the story.

And each year in this country, we go through the same argument. How can a game be allowed to dominate so? For those who have no interest – and, believe it, there are people even on this tiny lake who do not know which teams are left – it seems baffling to them that the national news should have to wait for overtime. Perhaps if they knew that Peter Mansbridge was as caught up in the games as anyone, they would be a little more understanding.

And as for those who have recently argued that the CBC should get out of sports entirely, so it can devote more air time to such matters as culture, what is culture but something that cuts across an entire nation as nothing else?

Of course, there is more to life than this.

This evening, for example, a vicious "summer" storm made the fireworks seem like little more than a flick of a match. Word has come in from town that a huge maple has squashed the grandmother's old house on Lorne Street.

And suddenly the power is out all over.

How will we eat? one of the kids wants to know.

Eat? Who cares?

How will we watch – or, even better, listen to – the game?

Part Two

~

Home Advantage

AND SO BEGINS the long season of Competitive Waiting. No one truly appreciates how difficult it is to be in Competitive Waiting, and this is partly because no one involved in it ever talks about it in public.

They speak of how well Jason is doing on defence, how Laura did at the regionals, how Matthew dives, Sarah swims, Sean tumbles, Jessica skates – but never, ever of how well *they* are doing in the sometimes sweaty, often frozen world of parental waiting and watching.

It is, in itself, an art so highly developed it is passing strange that The Sports Network hasn't thought to turn Competitive Waiting into its own spectator sport, complete with rules and scoring and playoffs.

Think of the possibilities. Imagine the sponsorship opportunities: hockey practices brought to you by Dixie Cups; soccer games brought to you by K-Mart lawn chairs; the pool, brought to you by Oxygen.

For those who may be just moving into Competitive Waiting this season, there are certain standards to maintain and protocol to be observed. The waiting is often as peculiar to the game as the playing itself.

Hockey:

The Canadian Hockey Association knows it destroyed a beautiful experience back in the '60s with its "Don't send your child to the arena, take him" campaign – but it also knows that the centre line will vanish before the parents will.

That being the case, those new to Competitive Waiting should know that the men are expected to stand at all times, either with their faces in the glass as close to the child as possible or, better yet, in a scruffy police lineup along the top row of the stands, backs to the wall, jackets open, and legs at all times wide enough apart to give the appearance of having once been on the rodeo circuit.

Women are not welcome in the wall lineup, but have been known to climb the glass to speak of pressing matters to player, coach, opponent, or referee. Most women, however, have the common sense to sit beneath a heater and talk about other things.

Those in Hockey Competitive Waiting should be extremely careful to have a clear fix on which parent belongs to which player, as this will avoid awkward pauses in the cutting up of weak players and incompetent coaches. It is also important to dress warmly – jackets with crests that give off the air of being an athlete are recommended – and a high tolerance for wretched coffee and spilled Slush Puppies is a must.

Figure Skating:

These are the quietest Competitive Waiters known to sports. They rarely, if ever, speak to each other. Those unlucky enough not to have brought thick novels or weekend newspapers are forced to wander lobbies, reading fire-escape messages and tiny, glaring plaques on old trophies. It does not look like a happy existence, which may have something to do with the cost.

Diving/Swimming:

Competitive Waiting is a bit of a misnomer in this sport; it might be better termed "Competitive Breathing." It is, after all, 115 degrees at pool level and rises one degree with every row of seats you climb. There is also just enough oxygen in the building to supply the earwigs that came in on the damp towels. Winners in this competition are, however, easiest to determine: those who pass out are immediately disqualified.

Soccer:

This is the antithesis of figure skating – easily and by far the most sociable of all waiting. The reason is simple: no one has the foggiest notion what is going on out there. And besides, they have been waiting since June for someone to score.

Baseball:

The problem with this sport, even more so than with hockey, is that each and every person involved in

Baseball Competitive Waiting once served as batting instructor for the Toronto Blue Jays. They are also the only ones on the field during T-ball who have the slightest interest in what is going on. (The players having properly determined that it is far more fun to build tiny mounds out of gravel, toss stones, pull grass, or even sit down with your back to home plate.) It does, however, have one distinct advantage over soccer: you get to go home when it rains.

Judo, Karate, Tae Kwon Do, etc.:

Competitive Waiting in these sports is distinguished by the fact that there is next to no resemblance between those waiting and those participating. A genetic resemblance, perhaps, but certainly not in ambition. The kids are happily learning such matters as poise and patience and fair play while those waiting are hoping for some neat little trick that will, once and for all, put a swift end to the bullies who've been jacking the family around since the Competitive Waiters themselves were in kindergarten.

Rhythmic Gymnastics, intramural sports, perhaps some others:

Competitive Waiting, here, is poorly developed, for the very good reason that the kids show up, the door closes, and the activity goes on. No parents allowed. Potential Competitive Waiters are thereby forced to go home or else look for an arena where the difficult art of sipping coffee and glowering at the same time can be practised.

The Future:

In an old-timer hockey dressing room the other day, a teacher wondered out loud what it would be like "if they put up plexiglass and let parents come into the classroom."

No one knows, of course. But TSN is most assuredly interested in buying the rights.

~

IT IS DARK – a cold, cracking evening in early January when the Christmas spirit has dwindled to a few twenty-five-watt strings along the far street.

I find her in my headlights as they sweep across the dark of the schoolyard, and she is running as fast as she can in the other direction, away. She is running with all the might that her young body can muster, her small feet finding the snow turns to fresh cement as she scrambles – a daughter fleeing in terror from her own father.

Later, she will try to explain what it felt like, how the only sound she could hear was the machine gun of her own heart, and how she looked for a lighted porch but could find nothing but the night turning ever darker. But first it is the father who must explain. She knows that an older sister was coming to meet her as she walked home from a friend's after a heavy day of playing. But she could not know that her father, coming along from work,

would run into the older sister and decide to turn back
and offer a warm ride. But when those family headlights
fell upon the child they were seeking – blinding her so
she could make out neither the car nor its driver – they
did not offer a ride but a threat that had been building
for weeks.

In the month leading up to Christmas, in this area and
in several other neighbourhoods across this sprawling
city, a car had pulled up to a child walking alone and an
overly friendly man had leant out, offering money, candy,
a ride. So far, there had been only the offers, followed by
wisely bolting children, but the incidents had been
written up in the papers, talked about in the classroom,
and, at one point, notices had even been sent home from
the schools.

Like all of her friends, she knew the surface details by
heart. These are imaginations, remember, capable of
spending an entire day turning a cat cage into a doll's
bedroom. Not even Stephen King could speculate on
what such minds might place behind the wheel of the
red car that had recently been observed with suspicion.

*"Will you walk me down? Will you come and get me?
Please?"*

It had got to the point where she would insist
someone stand at the front door as she travelled to the
very next house.

How strange to stand there, watching, participating
freely in such overblown fear. . . . You, who had

ridiculed a woman who came to visit in the summer and spent what should have been a lazy afternoon standing instead on a picnic table scanning a far tot lot with binoculars – a modern-day lifeguard making sure her children wouldn't drown in reality. How many times had you shaken your head in astonishment and gone into that well-worn speech about growing up where sweeping headlights and slowing cars meant the chance of a much-appreciated ride, where a certain retired gentleman would stand on the same corner each Easter and hand out candy to every child who passed by, where the only thing children were ever told to beware of was strange dogs . . .

A couple of weeks ago it suddenly didn't seem like the appropriate thing to say when, in another neighbourhood of this safe city, friends briefly lost their six-year-old boy. The mother of the friend he was visiting had called to say he had left, but he did not arrive until – after an hour of eyes feeling as if they were encased in lemon – a policeman delivered him home, safe and sound. The boy had merely taken the wrong turn on the street.

For weeks this terror of the red car continues until, with no further suspicious sightings, the notes cease and the talk turns to other imaginings.

On a bright morning she asks, again, if I will stand by the door and watch her go all the way next door. I tell her, once again, that this is getting silly. She walks to the end of the drive, stops, turns, and comes back, smiling sheepishly.

"You don't have to watch," she says.

"I know," I tell her.

But I stay there anyway, pretending to check the far clouds for snow, until I hear the sound of another door open and close.

~

THE ADULT measure of the day can be taken – even now, going on midnight – with nothing more than a quick glance at the laundry sink. The cheap plastic cowboy boots stick out over the sides of the sink as if he has somehow fallen in head first. But below the inverted boots there is only a muddy pair of corduroys, completely soaked, a shirt, completely soaked, a pair of underpants and a pair of socks, all completely soaked and draining. Only the child is missing.

He is upstairs, warm and dry, wrung out and strung out on the last of the Easter chocolate, and put to bed, finally, with his brief child's measure of the day – Great!

What the adult has seen of the day calls up other words.

There was the morning search for Band-Aids, the fight with the friend next door, the cat scratch, the fight to the

death with the youngest sister. There were two solid
hours somewhere around lunch in which he established
a new world record for asking, "What can I do?" And, of
course, there was the catastrophe – but more of that later.

"You promised," he says, the Band-Aids all placed, the
sisters wandered off to other battlefields, the cat outside,
the friend run off . . .

"Promised what?"

"We'd go for a bike ride."

Most nights for the past half-year or so it has been the
way he falls asleep. "As soon as spring comes," the parent
mindlessly says, "we'll get out on our bikes, okay?"

He thinks, now, that spring has finally come. The ther-
mometer is above freezing for the first time since the
Hundred Years' War. There are, for those who look
closely, bare and ugly patches along the side of the driveways. The air is strong with dog.

"You promised."

And so, off we go, tires spinning in the slush, brakes
laughing on ice. We are the first bikers of spring, two
lunatics heading off down a street where old men in
rubber boots still stand in their driveways with picks and
shovels, men who take the same satisfaction from clear-
ing pavement that small children find in lifting old scabs.

At the end of a distant street there is a bike path
heading off into nowhere. We are the first to break trail
through the seeping crystal. He falls several times. There
are, from time to time, clear breaks in the trail, places

where you can feel the early spring sun on your bald spot and think about the delights to come. Those are still a long way off.

He finds a curling indent in the snow that has been caused by melting around a branch and wonders if it could have been a snake we just missed. He looks for minnows in the brown water running off the fields. He slips on the ice, nearly loses a boot in the muck, bogs down on a slight hill. There is a thin triangle of mud and water up his back, thrown there by the rear tire. His arms grow tired pushing through the snow; he drops his bike in a puddle; he can't move another inch. There is a quarter-mile to go.

And all this is before the catastrophe.

Back home and changed, he heads out to see what has become of the schoolyard and thinks the ice that has formed over the ditch is as strong as it was last time he skidded over into the yard. He breaks through, the soaking as thorough as if he had, fully clothed, rolled off a dock.

He ends up at the door, shaking like the last leaf on the birch behind him, the water running loudly over the floor, the only warmth to be found in his tears. Ten minutes later, having run out of boots, he is back out again in search of more puddles, more mud.

An adult, who counts a day gone bad on nothing more than a cross look, heavy traffic, a stiff memo, an unexpected bill, a minor delay, would take a day like this and shudder. Yet the child who managed to shudder through this day has but one word for it: Great!

If only we could know what it is we lose along the way.

~

I SHOULD have seen it coming.

And perhaps if stretched Saran Wrap were not clear as air, I would have.

The first hint that there had been a dramatic change in humour about our house came very early one morning when I was doing what one usually does first thing in the morning.

The Saran Wrap — if it is not as clear in print as it is in reality — was wrapped tightly across the toilet bowl. Even if my eyes had been in focus, I would not have seen it.

The other hints came in rapid succession. I went to fill the kettle at the kitchen sink and they had already been there, as well. The nozzle on the sink hose — a strange contraption for which no one has ever figured out a use — had been Scotch-taped wide open and aimed so that, when I opened the tap, it shot out straight into my pyjamas.

I dressed in a shirt turned inside out on its hanger.

I stuffed my toes into shoes that were crammed tight with Kleenex. When I turned on the radio to pick up the weather, the volume was thunderous. I sat down and wept.

I wept for the days when *I* was the funny one, when I would rise in the morning and walk into a room where gurgles were coming from, and a small, drooling face would screech with delight if I did nothing more than turn my lips into an outboard motor.

I wept for those times when they would shriek the moment I came in from work, tiny bodies hurtling at their own personal home-entertainment centre.

At one point I could bring down the house with nothing more than rolling my eyes back into my head and sticking out my tongue. But no more, no more . . .

They speak of the stages of life, but they never talk about humour. They talk of size and maturity and adolescence and adulthood, but never about when the jokes change and when the stage switches from parent to child.

For a long time – forever, it seems then – you are the funny one. It is the sweetest ego builder of your entire life when you, who can never remember a joke long enough to bring it home, are briefly a riot merely for making odd noises and weird faces.

For a time – shorter, thank God – they are the funny ones. It is also sweet, but also wearing. It takes a very long time for them to understand that jokes must be fresh and that repetition can kill a good stage act faster than any-thing else.

Then there is the joke-book phase when they are the funny joke-teller – only the jokes are not theirs. They sit behind you during drives and read aloud, and so long as you can keep it in mind that you must guffaw every time they pause, it is possible to enjoy your own thoughts while they are reading, for the six hundredth time, awful puns on food and ghouls and animals.

And then, of course, there is the practical-joke stage, where we are at this very moment. It is the worst, and, one hopes, the briefest. Some, alas, never grow out of this stage; most mercifully do.

It will take a month or more of punching a hand down through the toilet bowl to see if it first bounces off Saran Wrap, but eventually the prank will be forgotten.

The two who are doing this – don't worry, we have their names, we know where they live – are a girl and a boy who will, over time, enter the next stage of humour in which their two older sisters have been for some time now.

This is when nothing is funny – particularly fathers.

And it is why some of us weep for those times when we were the source of all humour rather than the brunt. It is why even today when finally they are all asleep, some of us will stand a while at their bedroom doors listening to them breath and snore and toss and sometimes talk in their sleep.

And why, when we look at them and they cannot see us, some of us will, standing alone in the dark, still roll our eyes back into our heads and stick out our tongues. And remember when we were the stars of the show, the ones who had 'em rolling on the floor instead of the ones who had to mop up the floor.

~

THE PARENT is lying flat on the floor, his arm stretched as far as it will go, and his fingers are dancing nervously along the far corner of a very dark closet.

He is searching for something that, no matter how hard he fights to prevent it from happening, will cause his heart to skip, his skin to crawl – but which will finally, thank goodness, put his imagination to rest.

There is, unfortunately, no other way to look for a snake.

This wasn't supposed to happen. This was supposed to be a quiet weekend, involving nothing more than a clean basement and a fine fall walk through the woods.

That, anyway, was The Plan. The basement fought back. And the walk in the woods took an unexpected twist.

The Plan, of course, was to involve as many of your own kids as possible. Unfortunately, parents take forever to learn that family togetherness operates on a scale directly opposite to the family's cumulative age: the more interesting they get to be around, the less interested they are in being around you.

So in the end the walk involved the dog, the parent, and the youngest kid, who would only come along if two of his friends could as well – people he could talk to about something other than how lucky he is to have the opportunity to take a course or play a sport every night of the week.

The walk went well. There were trails to run and just the right number of easily recognizable birds for the adult to point out and remind them how fortunate they were to be able to go for a walk in the country and not have to worry about guerrilla warfare or poisonous snakes dropping out of the trees.

"A snake!" one of them suddenly yelled.

From where the parent stood he couldn't even see it, but the snake's progress was easy to trace. Boys jumping, crouching, jumping again, until, inevitably – "Got him!"

It was a small garter snake, probably out for its last slither before heading down between the rocks to a deep hole where it would then ball up with a dozen others to pass the winter in peace.

All this, of course, was explained carefully to them in that gnawing adult voice that has yet to chew through a single young eardrum.

But the snake had to go home; it had to be shown.

When will you let it go?

"Tomorrow – we promise."

Perhaps it was the fall air that weakened the adult. Whatever. . . . He agreed.

The snake had a lovely visit. It was given a name – Speedy. It played in the old doll house – "Come and see Speedy go down the stairs!" It crawled in pockets, frightened at least one kid in the neighbourhood and enthralled the rest.

The kids found a garage sale down the street, where an aquarium with a screen top was going and where the young man selling it had successfully kept lizards. They said they had enough money but were easily talked out of it. Better to save your money; it's only one night; and besides – the cage is for lizards.

But eventually, Speedy had to find some place to spend that one night. They built a cage and tied down some old cheesecloth across the top, and it appeared to work. He seemed happy. He looked as if he had already gone to sleep. Then, just before dark, a kid with a fearful look appeared at the end of the armchair.

"Speedy's gone."

Whatdya mean he's gone?

"We can't find him anywhere."

It took three searches through the moss and rocks of the cage to confirm he was not there. It took a single check of the rotting cheesecloth to find out how he'd gone.

He had to be in the kid's bedroom. He had to be. The only thing to do was throw the kids out and let the two adults go to work. First, shake out the sleeping bag from the sleepover. Not there. Then check under the bed. Not there. Then the toy box, the dirty clothes, the closet – he had to be in the closet, probably back there in that dark corner. Nothing to do but reach and . . .

"Got him!"

The call came from far away. The adults ran out of the kid's room and met the ten-year-old girl walking out of the adults' bedroom, Speedy draped happily on her arm.

Where was it?

"Hiding behind the drapes."

The adult does not know whether it was luck or not, but the screened aquarium down the street was still for sale, and it would, after all, save a marriage. The purchase was made, brought home, and Speedy put away safely.

But in the morning they were determined to let him go as promised, and promises, adults keep saying, must be kept.

They took him back to the same bush, kissed him (as God is my witness), and yelled their farewells as he crawled back under the rocks with a story to tell that should keep the other snakes burning with envy for as long as winter is cold. ("You ever been in a doll house?")

"Are you going to miss him?" the adult asked as they walked back to the car.

"No way."

"We're getting lizards."

Lizards!

"That's what the cage is for – you said."

~

THERE IS something about the location and the silence that tells you something is wrong.

Two other boys have come over to play. They are all upstairs in the boy's bedroom, silent, instead of down-stairs in the basement, screaming.

They are, obviously, not playing floor hockey, which is what they do in the basement. Nor Nintendo, which is what they do in the living room. Nor are they telling stupid jokes or fighting, which is what they do wherever they are.

But they are rarely in the bedroom – and never silent. A sensitive parent would prepare a herbal tea, sit down, and gloat quietly to himself about a child maturing and the possibility that they are up there reading.

But not this parent. This parent knows when some-thing is wrong. And this parent is more sensible than sensitive.

Which is why the old-fashioned, sensible parent tip-toes up the stairs, creeps along the hall, and rips open the door with a commanding "What's up in here?"

The room seems unreal. No lights on. A computer screen with an eerie green glow, quickly fading. The boys' cheeks with an eerie red glow, quickly rising.

A finger stabs a button, the computer off and a light on. "Just fooling around," they say. One giggles.

"Let's go play hockey," one suggests.

They fly out of the room, one still giggling.

It has always struck me as odd that the parenting handbooks never have a chapter on "snooping," for this, as much as driving and comforting, is part of the true art of bringing up the young.

There is, for example, a disk still cooling in the computer. The machine is an ancient school Apple IIc, the computer equivalent of the coal-driven steam engine, and it had been lying dormant for more than a year in storage before the boys hauled it out, plugged it in, and began looking for new games on the box of pirated disks that had come with this wrong-headed second-hand purchase.

The computer takes a while to warm up, the screen a while to form, but when it all comes together the screen is split into two cartoonish drawings of women in cheese-cake poses. One is called "Suzi," the other "Melissa."

The game itself is called "Strip Poker."

It takes another afternoon – the kids conveniently off at school – to snoop to the bottom of this. The game was somehow in the box, somehow missed by diligent parents. The boys had figured out how to start the game up but could not play it properly, a problem they solved when one brought a Rummoli board from home with all the poker hands illustrated in descending order of value.

Since then, Suzi and Melissa had been giving a computer course on female anatomy.

The sensible parent, fortunately, has been through all this before, many times. There are, after all, three older sisters. And one of the sharpest – if not fondest – memories is of the day we found one of them sitting at the kitchen table drawing pictures of enormous human appendages.

To handle that properly, we went out and rented a video called *Where Did I Come From?*, an animated production that is supposed to save the parent the time usually put aside for such awkward discussions.

The film, we soon discovered, involved hundreds of little sperm – "Cute," the then eight-year-old said – swimming up a pink channel toward a frilly-dressed egg, then breaking for some synchronized swimming to classical music.

It made slightly less sense, we decided, than getting pregnant from toilet seats.

Which explains, in part, why the old-fashioned, sensible parent decided to forget he had ever ransacked the bedroom looking for clues to the silent gatherings that had been taking place there for days.

And why, somewhere in the midst of a box of old computer disks, Suzi and Melissa are still fully clothed, awaiting only a royal flush to satisfy the curiosity of three boys.

And after that, if there are still any questions, the sensible parent is more than willing to take them.

~

IT IS FRIDAY night, a warm and pleasant evening pinched between an uncomfortably hot day and a wild, oncoming cloudburst.

We have come here to this hilltop campsite to indulge the fantasies of the young boy who is lunging, at the moment, straight at my heart with a wooden spear.

The boy is as pale white as the moon that will later emerge from the clouds. He has come here with a friend who is as white as the last few trilliums still blooming in the woods, and they are both wearing leather headbands with red feathers standing high over their short-cropped, pale hair.

The headbands cost three dollars each, the spear cost five dollars; eight dollars in total for another world, a world they have entered willingly and will leave reluctantly, their headbands to be later placed on a night table during the sleep-over, the spear standing guard over the dreams of two suburban boys who have just come from an Indian powwow.

But before the cloudburst sends everyone home, the dream can be enjoyed with eyes open and shared with a friend. The two boys are, in their own and each other's eyes, the first people of this country, brave hunters and wood wise. They read nothing into the smiles of those legitimate first people who have come here to this hilltop campground to dance and visit and, when the opportunity arises, sell three-dollar headbands and five-dollar wooden spears to the two whitest kids in the park.

But what is the harm? This, really, is what the childhood imagination is for – to dream awake, to dream asleep, to pretend that all things are possible before age begins to argue that most things are impossible.

"Does it look right?" the one asks as he straightens the red feather in his leather headband.

It looks perfect.

It is Saturday afternoon – a hot, sultry afternoon at the end of a five-hour drive that has brought two fifteen-year-old young women from English Canada to Quebec City, the heart of French Canada.

We have come here for other reasons, but also to indulge in the fantasies of adolescence, which have nothing to do with life in the woods and everything to do with life in the city.

And what city could offer more to such dreams than Quebec on a day like this, with the sun high over the ramparts and the boardwalk toast on bare feet and the walkways filled with ten thousand young visitors and locals working on their tans and their walks and their laughs and the best way to sit and stare off over the water as if Leonard Cohen were about to begin speaking from your mouth?

The air is filled with the sound of guitar and singing and everything tastes of ice cream, and muscles seem to shimmer in the combination of sunlight and suntan oil and there are fashions to die for – but that does not even hint at what may lie around the next corner.

Around the corner there are street artists teasing and waiters open to young Ontario women trying their second language, and at the corner the handsome calèche drivers want to know where they are from and whether they have seen this or that and what they think of the city.

Down the narrow streets there are small doorways leading to apartments with balconies holding flowers and chairs with astonishing views of the water and the streets filled with astonishing people walking by.

Here is where we will live. Here we will go to school. Here we will meet the ones destiny is unfairly holding back for the moment.

"Do I look all right?" the one asks the other before heading back out for the evening walkabout.

You look perfect.

It is Sunday evening, a hot, wet evening with the windshield wipers droning and the tires on the pavement like cold water splashing on a hot stove.

In the backseat, their imaginations stuffed with Quebec City, the fifteen-year-old and her friend are asleep. Four hours away a young brother is also asleep, his head swimming with headbands and spears.

There is nothing to do but let the adult mind drift, and dream, and fantasize.

If only there were garages that didn't charge $965.86 to fix the leak in the power steering.

If only the muffler will hold out till the end of summer.

If only the garden would plant itself.

If only Alexander Graham Bell had invented something to do with privacy instead.

If only things would slow down.

If only kids could sign up for things within biking distance.

If only roofs lasted fifty years instead of twenty-five.

If only lottery tickets were guaranteed.

If only tomorrow weren't Monday.

How truly perfect things would be for us all . . .

$$\sim$$

YOU ARRIVE at the regular time. You call it routine for some stupid reason, but it is rarely the same.

This day, when you come at the usual time, they are not even standing by the school doors, waiting for the minivan parade. Nor are they lingering by the gymnasium, taking their typical sweet time packing up their bags to go.

This time she is nowhere in sight, and when you finally track her down she is huddled with two of her young friends by a far drinking fountain, and it is clear when you turn the corner that they are not talking about water quality.

Whatever the topic was, you killed it instantly. And since you long ago lost your fluency in adolescent hand signals, there is just no picking it up again.

The next you hear about it is in the car, during the routine drive home.

She wants to know if you will get mad if she tells you something. You lie easily, of course; by this point you would pay her to squeal.

It is about one of the friends around the fountain.

"She thinks she's going through puberty."

You try to take this calmly, hoping the streets are dark enough that no one will notice the tire marks over that last lawn.

They have been reading one of those books so thoughtfully put out by those who believe they can make a bundle off parents who haven't the guts to talk about life to their own children. This particular book explains the mysterious changes that come to all boys and girls, and, at one point, suggests two sure hints of oncoming puberty are cramps and tiredness.

These young gymnasts, who have just spent an hour

and a half contorting their bodies, have put two and two together and come up with sixteen.

"And she's afraid to tell her mother."

Good, then that's the end of it. All is well in suburbia.

"I said you'd tell her."

This you try and take calmly as well, trusting that no one heard the scrape as you veered into that last parked minivan.

The fountain agreement was simple: one friend needed help, one friend volunteered help. To them it made perfect sense. After all, the parent who would happily do the dirty work was forever saying things like, We can talk about anything you want. You know that, don't you? . . .

You ask for it, you're gonna get it. The fountain agreement also included a proviso. The child feeling tired – and therefore, according to the book, on the verge of a full-blown sexual explosion – would go home and try to bring up the impossible topic.

If she couldn't do it, she would call, and the parent who brags he can talk about anything would make the call for her.

And all would be solved.

Back home there was little to do but fight the urge to pile into the Scotch that has been waiting for precisely such a moment since a visitor left it behind in 1983 – and wait for the call.

Unfortunately, in this home, that is about the length of a deep breath. The calls come in for the older ones and the youngest one. The calls come in from the carpet cleaners and chimney sweeps who do nothing but work in this neighbourhood. But nothing, so far, for the one who is most expecting a call.

The parent had time to consider how this might be handled, but no matter how hard he thought, the worse it got.

He would, after all, be a strange middle-aged male calling a woman he does not know with the news that her daughter is entering puberty.

Does he do it quickly, and anonymously, and pray she doesn't have one of those telephones that display the guilty number?

Does he only make matters worse by explaining it is all a figment of their imaginations?

Does he fail his own child by doing what he feels like doing – rolling up into a small ball and whimpering?

This is what happens to those who go out of their way to present themselves as calm and rational and unbelievably sympathetic when in fact all along it has merely been a ruse to get them to open up with their secrets.

Some secrets you'd be better off not knowing.

On into the evening the phone barks like a mad dog, each call causing the volcano in the stomach to erupt a little higher.

Finally it comes, and as she gazelles down the stairs to take the call, you realize what you have known right from the start: You cannot do it.

"Okay!" she sings into the receiver. "Bye!"

By now you are on your knees, buckling.

But then she is running back upstairs, not even concerned that you have passed out on the floor.

"Well?" you shout after her.

"What?" she shouts back.

But this is not a topic for shouting. You chase after her, and have a quiet talk alone.

"She doesn't want you to call now," she says. "She doesn't think she's going through it any more."

"Good," you say. "Then I don't have to make the call?"

"No – but thanks anyway."

You smile. "That's what I'm here for."

~

IT IS A feeling as strange – yet even more frightening – as that very first day I walked them into the school, pried off their hand, and hurried, at least one of us in tears, for the front doors.

She stands in a long, snaking line that has not moved for thirty minutes. She has come, on a school day, to write the only test she has ever looked forward to: for her "365." She's here to get her driver's licence. And she wants to drive home.

I sit and wait and watch the line, but what I see – perhaps because mortal danger is but moments away – is her entire life flash before your eyes. The first step, the walker (all they have to do to make them legal again is install airbags), the tricycle, the first bike and training wheels, the $959,000 mountain bike that now sits unused in the garage . . .

She has, actually, driven before, but it seemed so innocent then. She drove on a dirt road at her great uncle's Saskatchewan farm, no one else on the road, a section-and-a-half to turn around in if she needed it. And she has driven up at her grandmother's cottage, backwards and forwards in the gravel pit, with soft sand on all sides to cushion a mistake.

But none of that ever prepared me for this. I am in my forties on my own driver's licence. I am fourteen when I wake up in the morning, perhaps twenty when I realize there is a job to go to and someone needs their jeans dried for school. Sometimes I even feel my true age, but I am never old enough to have a daughter driving, let alone two, yet she will be the second to try for her licence in less than two years.

I grow old, I grow old, I will soon see my car rolled.

The hours pass, and eventually she is coming out of a small exam room, bouncing, smiling, waving the most frightening document known to older humanity.

She is in the car and we are going home and I am congratulating her and smiling and thinking that, perhaps this summer on a cottage back road, I will let her find out what it is like to share the road with other lethal weapons.

"Can I drive home?" she asks.

I say nothing.

"Can I?"

Finally: "You don't know how."

"I can drive," she says. "I watch. I know what to do."

Watch. She knows what to do from watching. What of all the dozens and dozens of hours we spent with fathers and mothers and older siblings and cousins, bucking up and down fields and back roads while we learned what a clutch was? What of grinding gears so violently your father would look back to see if the engine was going to fly out the exhaust in a million broken springs and bolts and torn gaskets? You don't watch and learn – not when the result is to roar down a highway at one hundred kilometres an hour with another car going one hundred kilometres an hour in the opposite direction less than a full arm's-length away.

Apparently you do: she sits carefully, adjusts mirror and seat, clicks on seatbelt, stares at me until I do mine, moves it into "drive," and pulls away.

She drives, calm and possessed and happy, and I sit, outwardly calm but shimmying inside like a '52 Meteor. I had my first accident at her age, sixteen. I was in three other accidents that year as my friends turned sixteen. In one instance – one I must never divulge to her – two of us "borrowed" a car that was neither ours nor our parents', and, it's true, rolled it on a back road. The Sixties, remember.

With her it cannot help but be different. She will not learn from her sister but from an approved course – the insurance savings demand it. And thanks to the new graduated licence system, she cannot drive at night, cannot drive on major highways, and cannot take off with a friend her own age.

Thank you, government regulators.

She is driving remarkably well. She stays to her own side, and, as we head up a quiet rural stretch of road, she passes other vehicles without flinching.

"How come you're such a good driver?" I ask.

She seems miffed by the question.

"I play a lot of video games, you know."

Of course. Of course.

The Nineties, remember.

~

IT IS OFTEN said – perhaps because it has all been done in public – that a politician has had a bad week. Some politicians have years of them.

But parents have bad weeks, too. They don't, however, end up in the paper . . . unless . . .

This particular week began with a high wind and an unfortunate trip to the corner store.

Such trips are always difficult if you happen to be

accompanied by children. You go for milk and, more often than not, you have to be sent out again for the milk you forgot the first time.

The distraction comes from their screaming for treats, and though it is tempting to lie, invariably they get treats.

A parent, however, comes with a twisted conscience that will agree to almost any corner-store purchase that does not have "sugar" listed in the ingredients.

"Can I get a kite?" the boy says.

He has it in his hands. His sister has a chocolate bar, a left-over Easter egg, and a mittful of rubbery candies that have been rolled in dental appointments.

The kite makes eminent sense – as a purchase.

"Sure. Why not?"

An hour later, in a wind that would ground an airliner, you are out assembling a snapping piece of plastic that has four parts but no instructions. Worse, there are two strings. "Dual controls," the wrapper says, which presumably means twice the ability to make it do as you wish.

The problem is that this particular parent has never flown a kite. He has run a hundred times with a long string attached to plastic bees and the like, but he has never actually flown. Other parents stand happily beside children who appear to be skywalking nine-part kites with mile-long tails, but this particular parent can only run and drag and curse.

The dual controls will fix all that.

The boy takes it up first. Using both hands, he magically releases the string until the kite is bucking high over his head, but not high enough.

"Make it go higher," he says, handing over the dual controls.

Unfortunately, at this point the wind begins to swirl and the kite to dive. The parent begins to run to keep it afloat, the dog decides to help and, jumping, gets wrapped in one of the dual controls. The parent spins, trying to unleash the dog and sustain the kite.

Less than thirty seconds after taking over, the parent is wrapped so tight in string he can neither lift his arms nor take another step.

The oldest child is bored. She is a freak of nature, for all the genetic testing in the world would never determine why it is she is interested in taking things apart and seeing how they work.

Clocks are fun. Motors are wonderful.

Her father, who wonders what keeps the electricity from spilling out the wall plugs, lives in fear of these moments. Her little brother has said she can have his broken remote-control car, and now it is in a hundred parts and she needs me to hold onto four coloured wires she has taped to the ends of batteries.

The batteries are very hot.

"I'm not touching that!"

She looks at me as if I have gone insane.

"It can't hurt you."

"How do you know?"

"It's a 1.5-volt battery."

"What does that mean?"

She stares at me with that look that is issued only to fifteen-year-olds. Get a life, it says.

"Never mind," she says. "I'll get somebody else."

The second oldest daughter has homework. She is on the phone to a friend and they are doing their homework together.

"Can you help?" she asks as I pass on the way to the fridge.

"Glad to."

But the page is filled with the scribblings of those who visited this planet only once before moving on.

From memory, the question is: "Find the square root of $1/2 \times 32/55$ h $892/1001 - 9854/10777$ f 3.00079."

"Is that right?" she asks. She points to a number that has been rubbed out a dozen times.

I look for a calculator, find none.

"Looks good to me."

The youngest daughter has lost her jacket. Yesterday there were shouts and tears, and today, after she has checked the lost-and-found, there has been more shouting and more tears.

"I didn't lose it!" she says.

"Well, where is it, then?"

"I didn't lose it!"

"Well, somebody did!"

"Did you have it?" she asks.

The way things have gone this week, probably.

~

"DAAAADD?"

The call comes from the front door, where they stand knee deep in a swamp of muddy runners and neighbours' forgotten coats, where the fall leaves are piled higher on the tile than on the front lawn, and where they have just been ripped into for the usual morning crimes: lost mittens, missed homework, unnecessary kicks, and frittered time.

Slowly, "Daaa-aaaad?"

Sharply, "What?"

"Were you ever a kid?"

They giggle, as if it could not possibly be so. And little wonder, given that they are among the chosen children of the decade, small household *objets d'art* for whom absolute perfection has become but the lowest common denominator. For parents to expect so much, to demand nothing less than excellence from each child, they must themselves have come to Earth as full-grown and fully formed human masterpieces, unable to accept failure and bad behaviour and lack of commitment in their small charges because, of course, they have never encountered such flaws in their own lives.

It requires a moment for reflection.

On Monday, when I backed the six-year-old against the wall and threatened him with reform school for taking a hockey stick to the legs of a sister, it did not occur to me to admit to that day so many years ago when, finally, I had an older brother down near the slab pile and within reach of the axe, and how he still wears the scar of that moment on his elbow. No reform school was required, and today there's not even a single point levied against my driver's licence.

On Tuesday, when the six- and the seven-year-old demanded they be allowed to quit school, they were treated to the standard lecture on how the law will keep them there until they are sixteen. And even then they would be fools to quit, for school is not only necessary and good for them, it is the only proven path to the sub-urban bliss to which all sensible children should aspire. Not a word was said of the three days I once spent hiding from Grade 6 in Mr. Gerhardt's blacksmith shop, sitting with his blessing behind a pile of scrap iron while the teacher thought I must be sick and parents believed all was well and fine.

Were you ever a kid?

Perhaps if full disclosure applied to parenting as well

as politics, a question like this would never need to arise.

When the ten-year-old comes home with a note about missed homework, it is treated like a subpoena. Nothing is said about my brother who, throughout a seven-year high-school career, refused to go to school on Tuesdays and yet today is a happy, successful parent who undoubtedly keeps such stories from his own children.

When the most talkative of the girls has been moved to four different seats since school began a month ago, she hears only of the disappointment felt, nothing of the thousands upon thousands of hours her father spent in detention rooms under forced silence. And when one of the girls packs a small suitcase for running away, she is told only of the dangers that lurk out there, never of that treasured day back in Grade 4 when her father and his best friend packed up enough Oreos and bananas for a year, turned their bikes down toward the railway tracks rather than the schoolyard, and left to make their own way in the world.

Somehow, we got back. And somehow – though I am still at a loss to say exactly how or why – it all worked out just fine. You mess up; you survive. At least that's the way it used to be before Nothing Less Than Perfection would do.

Slowly, "Were you?"

Sharply, "What?"

"Were you ever a kid?"

"Of course I was."

They are laughing – and they are still not out the door!

Sharper, "What's so funny about that?"

All together: "You were a *baby goat*?"

That's ridiculous. It's obvious I didn't turn into a goat until much later in life.

~

I T IS A situation only another parent of a near-teen will appreciate.

They will understand how one of their kind came to be parked in the dark corner of a school parking lot on a Friday night. And they will know instinctively what it is to see a hand lash out to knock off your stupid ugly toque, the same hand that now, quickly licked, is frantically trying to flatten your grey hair, which curls absurdly up over the ears in a fashion once sported by Clarabelle the Clown.

The hair of a parent, the hand of a child.

No, not a child. Not any more. The hand belongs to a daughter racing toward thirteen, a young woman who has just realized that she has no choice but to have her father – him, the stupid ugly old fool driving this disgusting-looking old van – walk her across the black schoolyard to the door of the school itself.

There is supposed to be a dance going on here. A

pre-teen dance. A tribal ceremony in which the hormones of Grades 6, 7, and 8 will gather in a ritual that involves pretending they are orphans who drove here themselves in new Lamborghinis, drove here straight from Hollywood with the only copy in the world of the latest alternative music CD, and will be leaving tomorrow for a Caribbean swimsuit shoot for *Elle* magazine.

There are no fathers in such a world. No mothers, no brothers, no sisters, no rides, no rules, no curfews – and there is most assuredly not any understanding that anyone must be ready and waiting right at the front doors at exactly 10:30 p.m., when a disgusting-looking old van will pull up and flash the interior lights to reveal an old clown in a toque at the wheel, waiting.

But still, no one counted on this. There was panic enough in just being late. But now there is utter dread that this may not even be the right school. Perhaps it is even the wrong night. There are no lights on. No cars in the parking lot. Not even anyone jumping out of a Lamborghini that is quickly whisked away by eager valets.

"Walk over with me," she says.

Of course, once the hair is plastered down.

Don't take a hand. Don't even try to walk abreast. A bit behind, a bit more – close enough to help if needed, far enough away not to be related if seen.

Walking by the gymnasium, a loud, thudding beat comes through the brick, and that is all a creature of the night needs to hear. She is gone, running ahead, bolting for the school doors and psychologically bolting the dancehall doors behind her.

Out in the schoolyard the parent finds he is lingering by the revolting van. There are northern lights high above the schoolyard and not even the thud of the beat at this distance.

But then a door bursts open. The night barks with the sound of rap, then snaps silent again as the door closes. A kid has just come out for air.

More to the point, he has come out for a smoke. He is twelve. Maybe. He is short. He is so skinny it hurts. But as he moves into the light spilling from a far window, it is apparent he may fill more space per square pound than any human in history. He walks as if a horse moves beneath him. His arms dangle as if he has pillows stuffed into his armpits. And when he lights up, it is as if every lesson ever passed on by Bogart and the Duke and Jimmy Dean has been learned to the point that he has turned himself into a perfect study of what it is to be twelve years of age.

Another door opens and shuts, this time on the far side of the gymnasium. Two slim figures begin circling each other. The light is dim, but the intention only too obvious: this is a fight.

The parent does not know what to do. He stands, watching, wondering how he should react, when suddenly the two bodies charge each other, the distance closing with the happy screech of a very young woman.

The parent hadn't even realized it was a boy and a girl. He had grown so stupid so fast that he had completely forgotten that tickling is the time-honoured trick the very young discover that allows them a first tentative touch at a mystery that will keep them spinning for the rest of their lives.

The stupid parent leaves, startling the young ticklers with the sound of the door, and they hurry back in as he pulls away in a van that tells everything about him they will ever need to know.

Two hours later he is back for the pre-arranged pickup. Parents have a choice in how this is done: they can go in and wait at the gym doors, or they can wait outside. But no matter which option is selected, the rules remain the same – no one knows anyone else.

The kids come out of the gym with their heads down, moving in clusters. The parents who have gone inside stand staring at their goofy-looking galoshes.

Perhaps the kids note the galoshes, perhaps the parents recognize a fluorescent lace – who knows, all that is certain is that eventually a pair of related galoshes and runners head out the door together, their distance carefully kept, and eventually, in silence, they find themselves getting into the same vehicle.

The parents outside sit in idling cars as if waiting for a scheduled ferry. They sit like tourists afraid of being caught out, as if the stream of exiting children are all strangers from another land, which in a way they are.

And it is still one of the enduring mysteries of humanity how the departing eleven- and twelve-year-olds, not one of whom ever looks up, are able, on instinct alone, to find their way to the revolting vehicle that brought them here and was instantly erased from their minds.

~

SITTING HERE on the verge of criminal activity, I can hear the kettle calling for action.

In a few moments – presuming no one with a badge and handcuffs hears the whistle – I shall walk out into the hall and pick up the morning mail before heading for the kitchen.

It is mail that should be going out, not coming in, and it is a letter neither sent by me nor sent to me, and yet in a short while I will be sitting beside the kettle – forehead hot and damp as the spout – and I shall be steaming open this letter and reading it and, perhaps, resealing it, but perhaps first rewriting the contents to suit my own purposes.

May my judge be another parent, for forgiveness of such a clearly criminal act is only something one in potentially similar circumstances could fully appreciate.

My daughter has written my boss.

Why she has done this I do not know, but there on the

cluttered table heading into the cluttered hall is a sealed envelope, the address one to which I drive almost every day, the return address mine, the letter organized perfectly, the stamp the right price and the flag the right side up.

There is no doubt that it is written by her. She is of that age when the letter "i" is dotted with a heart; she is of an age when you can still read what she writes.

What is entirely in doubt is what she has to say and why she wishes to say it. Her Grade 6 teacher, bless her heart, has spent much of the year on letters, and, so far, they have written to pen pals and cousins – but I cannot for the life of me imagine a homework assignment where they have been told to write to their parent's boss.

I work for a newspaper, and it is a rule of thumb that when people like what you have to say they write to you, and when they despise what you have to say they write to your editor. Perhaps she has misunderstood my intentions when, each morning, I grab for the letters-to-the-editor page and, rapidly hyperventilating, search frantically for my name. Perhaps she has thought I hoped to find it there.

I am also deeply concerned about my own mouth. For the better part of the morning, I have been sitting here thinking about what I might have said about my work and my employer over the past weekend, and – if other parents were to sit down and do the same, they would also discover – the potential is devastating.

There is no doubt she would have been told this weekend that I am being worked to death by very sick people who could care less if I suddenly curled up into the foetal position and began eating the contents of my briefcase instead of, as she had hoped, spending the afternoon letting her hamster run in and out between my shirt buttons.

She would also have been told, perhaps even in a rather high-pitched screaming voice, that I have not got so much as a dirty penny to my name and that there is no way on earth she will ever, ever own Barbie's Rain Forest.

It being a weekend, she will certainly have heard that we can't afford a car that doesn't stall at lights, that we will not be going to Florida this year or next year or the year after, even if she and her sisters and brother are willing to hitchhike down and sleep in open fields.

And if she listened-in last night while the only adults in the house lingered over pizza, she will have heard that I am underappreciated as well as underpaid, and that I, like everyone else I know and admire, have been jacked around and taken for granted for all too long now and that I'm not about to lie down and take it any more . . .

Wait! She is at the door, coming from a hard afternoon of messing up the neighbourhood.

"Did you see my letter?" she asks.

"Letter?" I ask absentmindedly, pretending to hurry toward the kettle with an empty coffee cup.

"See?" she says, holding it up.

"Oh?" I say, pouring from the kettle, "That's my work, isn't it?"

"Will you mail it for me?"

Now is my chance: "Sure, what's in it?"

"I've done a comic strip."

I stand there blowing over the coffee, afraid to ask "On what?"

~

"DID GRANDPA have an earring when he was young?"

An interesting question. I suppose I could say I wasn't there, and couldn't possibly know, but this is hardly one of those times when you really had to be there – if you know what I mean.

I doubt very much that he had one when he worked in the bush camps. I doubt he wore one when he took the train out West to bring in the harvest. I have a faded picture of him as a young man on the Eganville senior hockey team, 1927-28, and while he and his teammates all have slicked down hair, none would appear to be wearing an earring, no.

You don't see a lot of earrings with the huntin' 'n' fishin' set.

"Did he?"

"No . . . no, I-I don't think he did . . ."

The grandson has one, though, a small golden stud in one ear that wasn't there when he woke up this morning.

It's hard to explain what happened – harder still to explain what happened to me – but let it be said that there are times when this world spins so fast it makes you silly.

He had been talking about an earring for a year or more. His cousin Howie – a big, macho junior hockey player – wears one, used to wear three. A lot of the rock singers he likes wear one. And this year the new Big Man on campus (grade-school version), a kid named Stanley, has both a stud in his ear lobe and the starting goalie job on the rep team.

Why would he not want one?

Still, it was something considered fine to talk about so long as it was far off in the future. As the father of one of his best friends says, "You can get your ear pierced the day you move into your own apartment." End of discussion.

That is the essential difference between hardline parents and flakes. And if I may speak for the flakes, things happen.

In the morning, the second daughter announces she has saved up enough babysitting money to stop at the beauty salon on the way home from school and get her ears pierced. Her father, the flake, points out that she already has her ears pierced. She points out that the new style is two earrings in each ear.

She is asked about the boys. It seems, to her, a pretty dumb question. She lists off the boys who have earrings. She cannot think of one who does not.

All this, of course, is overheard by the boy. No one notices him hurrying up to his room to count up his loonies.

The flake is at work when the phone call comes. The boy has counted his money and talked his mother – who has never before been considered a flake – into taking him to get his done.

Get what done?

"His ear. He's got the money."

The question that thunders through the flake's brain cannot be asked. Which side? He remembers hearing a thousand times in the past that there was something about the side chosen that meant something important, but he cannot remember exactly what, or, for that matter, which side is considered the safe side.

He begins driving home, the foot falling ever harder on the accelerator until, by the time the neighbourhood mall is in sight, people are racing outside to see what the tire squealing is all about.

He runs inside, skidding past the grocery store, and comes puffing to the door of the beauty salon, where hangs the sweetest message imaginable: Closed.

The flake sags, grateful, only to find that behind the sign the last customers of the day remain – a small boy among them.

The door opens and the flake goes in, shouting "Which side?"

The beautician looks up, puzzled.

"Which side did you put it on?"

She smiles and points to the boy's beet-red ear, where a small stud flashes. "That one."

The flake has no idea how to word the next question. He cannot ask what that side means. He cannot make yet a larger fool of himself.

The boy, calm and happy, has his eight dollars out. He smiles as if it is the best money ever spent.

Finally, the flake can hold back no longer.

"Do you always do the same side for little kids?" he asks, leading, begging.

"No," she says. His heart sinks.

"I used to be in Kitchener," she says, smiling. "All the kids down there pick the other side."

"I got the same side as Stanley," the eight-year-old says.

The flake says nothing. Inside, he is on his knees, praying, making mental notes not to move to Kitchener.

Later, when the ear is not so red – and, for that matter, neither is the flake – the eight-year-old is still talking about it.

"Won't grandpa be surprised!" he says.

"You bet."

~

WHEN IT IS over – when it has finally turned out exactly the way you hoped it would, prayed it would, when you were running around in a total, absolute coldsweat panic – you can only think about how fast it happens.

One moment you are lining up at the pool with a ten-dollar bill in your hand, the little boys heading to the change room to the right with you, the one little girl heading left with a squeal and a promise to be there first.

A moment later – though it feels like precious hours lost – you are on the telephone to the police and you cannot remember what she was wearing or how tall she is, or, for that matter, what your very own daughter looks like.

Panic does strange things to the human body, but it does nothing so well as throw blame.

How could this happen? How could you now not even be certain that she went through the change-room door? When you had stood around watching the boys dive for a while and finally thought to go and ask one of the young women lifeguards to check the change room for her, how much time had been lost by your dithering, your not wanting to embarrass yourself by appearing too over-protective, too much the parent whose common sense has been twisted out of control by newspaper head-lines and imagination?

Only hours ago you had been ridiculing, as usual, others who can't imagine their child heading off to the corner store on their own, who would, if they could, outfit their child with cellular phone, guard dogs, Chubb alarm system, Mace, whistle, flares, and tracking device before letting them go to the refrigerator during a commercial break.

And now here you are, sputtering over the telephone to the police.

The lifeguard was in too long checking the change room. Before she even came out, you knew no one was in there. And after you double-checked and triple-checked the pool, you knew something unbelievable, unimaginable had gone wrong.

Maybe she just went home, the police suggest.

She wouldn't. Her bike's still leaning against the fence.

She probably walked over to the mall.

She wouldn't.

They sit there, dialling your home number and letting it ring, you growing impatient, testy, because it is obvious she is not there to answer it. She is missing!

The air takes on a certain charge when this is finally said. There is something about the way people begin moving about, the way they run quickly to corners, their necks raised, their eyes darting. Without a word being said, it alerts all other adults until, in an instant, panic and curiosity and blame fill the air with a hot intensity beyond even the powers of a July sun.

A cruiser is on its way. Until it gets here, there is nothing to do but run around like a chicken with its head cut off.

When it is so early into the panic, you know it is a false alarm — but then, you also know that others felt this way when it first began for them, and soon the minutes became hours and then days, perhaps years, time becoming such a cruel factor that eventually you cannot decide whether it is better to know or better not to know.

You know this is going to turn out just fine because it always does. This has happened to you before. Many times. That time in the mall. Several times around the neighbourhood. But it always turns out all right. So this time it has to, too — right?

But even though it always turns out all right for you, the flash of a false alarm is all that is ever needed to know that there could be no pain like the one feared most.

And then, just as quickly as it happened, the nine-year-old appears, walking happily from the direction of home, swinging a small gym bag.

She recoils from those running at her, the one lunatic trying to hug her.

She brought her sister's bathing suit by accident.

She had to go home and get her own.

She couldn't take her bike. It was chained to yours.

She had told the girl taking the money. Whoops, the girl taking the money hadn't put two and two together.

There being nothing to do but swim and be stared at by parents who have never seen such absurdity, you pass once again through the change-room doors and, a few moments later, she emerges as she should have a half-hour earlier.

But this time, she is not speaking.

For the rest of the afternoon the nine-year-old girl dives again and again, breaking her stride only to curl her lip at a parent who has made an inappropriate fuss about nothing.

She sneers, dives, surfaces, sneers and dives again.

A small treasure, disappearing for as long as she can hold her breath. A nine-year-old in full possession of her own life, offering her own small opinion of a parent who thought he would have to hold his own breath forever.

~

YOU MUST never, the cardinal rule goes, try to live your life all over through your children.

The school teachers are on strike. She has already missed a week, and it is beginning to look like it will be a very long time before the high-school teachers go back in, if ever.

She says she'd like to go to the high school her parents attended.

At first it seems a ridiculous notion – the school, after all, is five hours away by car – but as the days plod on and the news worsens, it begins to make more and more sense.

Her parents' school is in a faraway board where there is no strike, and her grandparents have empty bedrooms and full refrigerators.

We have talked of this before, but never seriously. She has been told, for example, that the social ramble was so superior in this small-town school that her father stayed six years, as did an aunt, and an uncle seven.

She is old enough to be off on her own, and the notion has more charm to it than the teenage mind can imagine – almost as much, in fact, as the middle-aged brain can create.

She would not only learn more about those she should worship; we would learn about her.

She has, for example, been told a thousand times the proper way to walk to this school: up Lorne Street over the hill and down Florence Street rather than straight down Lansdowne and then up Brunel Road. The distance is exactly the same, but overachievers invariably went down first, then up, while those who had Saturday nights booked solid for the rest of their lives first went up, then down.

This is, then, an extraordinary opportunity for the parent to find how much she is like him.

The appropriate calls being made, the dream becomes reality. She is admitted to the distant, small-town school until the city school goes back in.

Three weeks later, the city school goes back in, so the transfer back is made.

But before the bags and tapes and guitar are all packed up for the return haul, she is asked to reveal which of the two routes she chose for the five-block walk to school.

"Neither," she says.

"Grandma drove me every day."

Her younger brother has seen another, older kid walking up the street carrying a lacrosse stick and a ball, his wrists rolling as he absentmindedly fakes out the fantasy world he is passing through.

"I want to play that game," he says.

This strikes the parent as worthy talk. Hockey season is finally over, the bills will soon be paid, and the psychotherapy sessions are coming to an end.

Besides, he knows lacrosse, which was the game of note back in the small town where you were defined by the way you walked to school.

Lacrosse is a very tough game, he is told. A lot rougher than hockey.

"I still want to play."

And so a league is found in the neighbouring town. A couple of sticks are found, and the parent begins to instruct the child in the intricacies of the game.

The child is warned to prepare himself. In the small town where this game mattered more than life itself, lacrosse once meant broken glasses and cuts and sore arms and scraped knees. Hockey is nothing compared to this insanity, he is told.

"I still want to play."

The team practises, and two weeks later plays its first game.

But it is no longer the same game. All the violence of lacrosse is now found in hockey. In lacrosse they call penalties and no one argues. In lacrosse the parents sit quietly in the stands, some of them reading, none of them frothing at the mouth. He plays, and the kids are laughing. A ball bounces into his stick, he fires it and the ball bounces into the net. Nothing to it.

"Fun," he says. "A lot easier than hockey."

Their sister wants to change her name.

This is something the parent can relate to. At her age he wanted the same. He would rather change his age now, of course, but at one point "Joe" sounded pretty good – anything but whatever it was you happened to have been saddled with at birth by those who didn't have the foggiest notion of who you really were by the time you became an adolescent.

She has been toying with "Marie-Theresa." She has been thinking of "Kristiana." But she doesn't know for sure.

What she wants right now is permission.

"Can I please change my name?"

If that is what you really want, she is told.

"Good, I think I'll go up and see what I look like now in the mirror."

ONE MIGHT have thought that in the age of subdivisions and renovations, it had become a childhood experience that would never again be found.

The Haunted House.

I was late hearing about this one – not being part of that remarkable network that includes recess and swinging tires and the backseats of minivans headed off for courses no one but parents would ever sign up for – and was let in on the secret more out of necessity than any sense of sharing some hot childhood news.

Where the story began, no one seems to know. But it did eventually hit the school, and a couple of upper-grade kids took a couple of lower-grade kids to see it, and by the time the boy rounded up some of his pals to investigate, they knew they had no choice but to invite me along.

The reason had nothing to do with risking life and limb to enter a haunted house. That they would happily do on their own. But they did need an adult to get them across the busy highway.

"Will you take us to the Haunted House?" they wanted to know.

"There's no such thing."

I said this certain there could be no such thing here in an Ottawa suburb where they put up historical plaques on houses that don't have the family room on the main floor.

Whatever these kids imagined might pass for a haunted house, I had to see.

After all, as for everyone born before they invented

bedroom communities and paint-stripping, the mere phrase "Haunted House" brought back a flood of memories:Vincent Price movies, eccentric old recluses, abandoned farmhouses where a ten-year-old could put up his feet and enjoy a nice quiet rum-dipped cigar.

The Haunted House was usually where you saw your first sunbathing magazine and then spent the next half-dozen years convinced that, the moment you became an adult, someone was going to come along and airbrush out all your weird parts.

"Let's go."

Off the four of us went by bike, down the street and across the busy road until, eventually, we came to a small industrial park and then a field.

"I see it!" the kid who had come earlier with his Grade 6 sister called out.

Off through the field they set, frantically pushing their bikes through mud and burrs and dead flattened grass until they came to a stand of scruffy pine half concealing a rundown and blackened farmhouse.

Whoever had lived here had clearly given up before bailing out. The shed, the yard, the house – even the outhouse – were filled with garbage.

Someone had taken an axe to the walls, stones to the windows. A couch had been burned and tossed. A refrigerator smashed.

"Fantastic!" one of the boys pronounced things.

"Can we go upstairs?"

"No!"

"Why?" – their question filled with ghosts and rotting bodies and blood-sucking bats.

"Because you might fall through the floor."

"Can we just go up and look?"

"No."

"Please . . ."

"Only look. Up quickly and down. And don't leave the top of the stairs."

Up they scrambled, eyes popping, each with a hand on another's T-shirt.

"Wow!" the first to arrive at the top of the stairs shouted.

"Somebody's been here!"

"They were smoking! And there's magazines – can we go closer?"

"NO!"

They froze.

"And get back down here right now!"

They scrambled back down, certain the adult had seen something slimy and blood-curdling that they had missed.

"W-w-what's wrong?"

"Nothing! We're going home!"

Off through the mud and burrs and dead flattened grass we went, over the busy road racing for home, the kids like explorers who had just discovered a great treasure.

The adult looking like he had just seen a ghost.

~

SOMETHING happened one morning this week that turned a growing hunch into an undeniable fact. I've become a social pariah.

It was early morning, cool with rain threatening, and pure chance caused the adolescent daughter and the aging father to head out the front door at exactly the same time, the daughter carrying her saxophone and headed for a schoolbus, the father with his briefcase headed for the downtown bus.

As chance would also have it, the house we were leaving is situated at the midway point of a curving suburban street. It is possible to turn left or right and head for the bus stop. And since it doesn't matter which way you go, you may as well go together.

"Which way are you going?" she wanted to know.

"Whatever way you want."

"You go that way."

There was no blood, but that does not mean there was no stabbing. The father stood blinking at the foot of the driveway where one road diverged; the daughter flashed a quick you-understand grin and turned left, leaving only the right open and the father to pretend he had to hurry to catch the bus.

This has been happening a lot lately. For a dozen years you are your child's shadow – two happy bodies dancing to the same gawdawful music, two mouths laughing at the same stupid jokes, two hands of different size that fit together tight as Russian dolls – and then suddenly you are completely out of synch with your own flesh and blood.

It is a bitter moment. Your hands catch by accident and you realize that the smaller has somehow outgrown the larger. It is the grip of fast-forming strangers, anxious to let go.

This has happened already. The two older girls are in the bathroom sculpting their latest look with hairspray and combs that work like pitchforks and you barrel in as you once did, grab the hairdryer, turn it on full, and pretend it has blown you down and is grinding your head into the linoleum. Once they laughed. Now they look at each other rather than you.

You walk around the house singing the refrain from *Tommy* at the top of your lungs, and they tell you to shut up, whereas not so long ago – say when the Beatles were in their ninth comeback – they would join in joyously. You scream back about the sacredness of The Who's music. But then you realize that you bought your copy of *Tommy* a quarter-century ago and still consider it state-of-the-art rock.

How did this happen? How does a parent turn instantly from his or her child's favourite toy into the child's curse?

I am puzzled as to whether they address this phenomenon in school. In health class, for example, when they talk about all the changes they are going through at this age, do they say the girls will develop breasts and the boys will grow strange hair, but that is nothing compared to what your hormones are going to do to your dad?

Dad's going to change pretty drastically. At the very

least, he'll be lurching around with green slime dripping from his nose. And every time one of their friends calls, he'll be greeting them at the front door with a complete symphony of disgusting body sounds.

He'll talk too loud, sing off-key, play ridiculous music, ask the most appalling questions in front of their friends, answer the telephone and – on days his hormones are completely out of control – actually wave to them if he happens to be driving by when they're walking back from school.

It happens. It has happened – and there's nothing anyone can do about it.

The youngest girl is at my sleeve. It is getting dark out, and she wants an escort down the street to Katie's. Will I please go with her? She doesn't say so, but the sense is there that she wouldn't even mind if one of her friends sees us.

Down the curving street the father and the third, and youngest, daughter go, the two of them holding hands and walking and talking happily, two friends for life holding onto each other in the dark.

The daughter holds on tight, not knowing what lurks around the corner.

The father holds on tighter, knowing exactly what lurks around the corner.

Part Three

~

Roots

I DON'T KNOW how old I was when I first learned that beer grows wild in creeks.

Maybe seven, maybe eight.

But I do know that I was into my forties when I discovered that my father had never seen mountains.

It was a realization that came about entirely by accident. My father and I were driving along Highway 3 where it runs through the Adirondacks near Childwold – just the two of us on a pilgrimage we had been talking about for years – when a sharp turn to the left put us in sight of 2,700 feet of soaring treeline.

"Is that a mountain?" he wanted to know.

"According to the map," I answered, reading and driving at the same time, "yes – Mt. Matumbia."

"Tch-tch-tch-tch-tch."

My father makes that sound when something is either very special or very off-putting. It stands for amazement, and in this particular case it was remarking on a life spent almost entirely in and around the gently rolling bush of Algonquin Park.

Apart from a few train excursions and a single plane trip to, of all places, Texas, he'd put in more than eight decades of visiting the world through books and radio, and finally – once the dreaded retirement question was finally answered by a skidding logging truck when he was seventy-three – the marvel of television. He could locate any mountain range you could name, but he'd never seen one.

My older brother and I first visited the world beyond Algonquin Park with him through the car radio. On a hot summer night he would grab a lantern and head off through a long dark path to the highway, where the Pontiac was parked. And here, when the clouds were kind, he would walk the radio dial through the static and the fading signals until he found the sounds of a distant ball game, with luck Mel Allen calling the Yankees, Red Barber doing the Dodgers.

We would sit, the windows often rolled up against the mosquitoes and the plastic seats sticking to our backs, and after he and Jim had debated, once again, who was the greatest player of the day – Mantle or Mays – he would often take the flash and head off into the tiny creek that ran along the road and return a few minutes later with a couple of cold green bottles, the slightly skunky smell of beer cutting through the citronella as he cracked the caps with his knife.

It seems slightly off to say in these oh-so-correct times, but it was sports and statistics and that meaningless but comforting talk about people we would never meet that formed the bonds between fathers and sons in those days. Slightly off but true all the same, and we hang onto it today no matter what the times, for what got us talking back then still gets a man in his eighties going in the morning. The standings, it turns out, are important.

He told us about once driving over to Hull in the fall of 1928 and seeing Ruth and Gehrig play an exhibition match during a rare barnstorm into Canada. He had a million names in his head – Home Run Baker and Walter Johnson and Rogers Hornsby and George Sisler and, of course, The Babe, always The Babe – and every time his eldest son would dare suggest that Mickey Mantle was Babe Ruth's equal, he had the same definitive response.

"Tch-tch-tch-tch-tch."

He took, and continues to take, enormous pride in his baseball knowledge. DiMaggio's 1941 season is as fresh in his mind as the current pennant race. He knew the numbers and he knew the players and he could, when the moment moved him, stand leaning against the door of the car on a warm summer's night when the mosquitoes were down and recite, from heart, Ernest Lawrence Thayer's "Casey at the Bat."

". . . Ten thousand eyes were on him as he rubbed his hands with dirt;

"Five thousand tongues applauded when he wiped them on his shirt.

"Then while the writhing pitcher ground the ball into his hip,

Defiance gleamed in Casey's eye, a sneer curled Casey's lip . . ."

Sometimes when he tells these stories – like the one about Ruth driving in the winning run at Hull – I am startled by how far he goes back. He remembers when the first car came to Eganville. He knew a man in Whitney who fought in the American Civil War.

"I used to be ashamed of my age," he says at one point on this trip. "Now I'm kind of getting proud of it."

I no longer remember how long it is that we have talked about one day going down to see the Baseball Hall of Fame. I do know that so much has changed. Today I drive. I control the radio. Mountains are old hat.

Both of us are now fathers of four children. But not much else is the same, not even the role. My generation talks about parenting as if it were a trade one has earned certification in. His generation didn't have time for reflection.

There were no vacations. And even if there had been, there was usually no car. Not poor, just typical. He worked five and a half days, fifty-five hours a week, and

Sundays were for putting in enough wood for winter. Our mother had even less breathing space, and, again, it was just typical.

But that doesn't mean there was none of what they now absurdly call quality time. There was time, plenty of it, and never more so than in the summer, when the family would move out into the Park to be closer to where he worked. We would fish with him, and listen to the game with him, and sometimes, when the kids were playing their strange baseball game where you had to run up a slanted tree to register a home run, he would come in from his work and pitch a few or just lean against the porch and watch and slowly roll and smoke a cigarette.

Almost everyone smoked back then. He still does, though I never did. Yet if I am truthful about it, there is still something about the first whiff of a lighted cigarette – especially when a wooden match is used – that reminds me of him. And though I hate the habit, I am hooked on the memories.

I have at least one child, now, who is mortified by my existence, and I suppose there was a time when my own father embarrassed me, though I do not accurately recall this sensation. He was far older than most other parents, but hard outside work kept him fit. And my friends liked him as a character, an adult who could joke and kid and sing and even play the harmonica.

And he taught us all the value of books. He read, and reads today, more than any person I have ever met. My brother and I have one precious memory of going into the mill to fish with him not long before he retired and finding him in a trailer without electricity, a dim coal-oil lamp on the desk and a translation of Plutarch on his snoring chest.

He passed on an inability to pronounce words. He once said his favourite books were about the maa-fay-ya, and it took us hours to figure out he was talking about the Mafia. My own head is filled with words I will let slide through the keyboard but never the mouth.

"What's that mean?" he asks as we pass by a cottage community on Otsego Lake.

"What's what mean?"

"That sign – 'Eee-zed Shop.'"

"No, no. That's 'Eee-zee Shop.' American pronunciation. Get it?"

"Tch-tch-tch-tch-tch."

He should have been exhausted by the time we reached Cooperstown, but he refused to go to a motel until he had seen with his own eyes the bats that Gehrig and Ruth and Williams and Cobb had swung and the balls that Walter Johnson had thrown.

He stayed until they closed the doors, an old man with a cane standing in front of the displays and remembering what he had read in the papers and heard on the radio, sights more vivid in his head than in the brightest of glass cases.

"I knew them all," he kept saying. "I knew them all."

When he came to the special section devoted entirely to the memory of The Babe, it was as if he was once again in Parc Dupuis over in Hull, a young man from the bush, shouting out the name of the great man from New York who had just won the World Series.

I stood against the far wall, not remembering scores or plays or players who now dance with the gods, but hearing again the sound of a creek and the sound a car door makes in a still night and the way a radio dial can connect small boys and their father to a world they will carry with them forever.

Later, in the souvenir shop, I showed him all the various versions of "Casey at the Bat" that were for sale and offered to buy him one, which brought back a look straight out of 1956.

"Tch-tch-tch-tch-tch."

"What do I need a book for?" he asked, tapping his temple. "I got it right here."

And heading off into the soft light toward the car, he proved it.

". . . Oh, somewhere in this favored land the sun is burning bright;

"The band is playing somewhere, and somewhere hearts are light,

"And somewhere men are laughing, and somewhere children shout;

"But there is no joy in Mudville . . . mighty Casey has struck out."

Not on this scorecard he hasn't.

~

SHE WANTS to know where the Chinese coins were put.

She wants to know if her kimono still fits.

She wants to take the little tea cups. The chopsticks. The fan. The bead necklace. The peasant hat.

"What are you doing with all this stuff?" you ask.

"Today's Heritage Day at school. We have to take in something from another country."

"But isn't Heritage Day supposed to be about where you're from?"

"Yeah."

"Well – who's Chinese around here?"

"No one. But it can't be from Canada. It has to be another country."

"You mean the country you came here from?"

"I guess."

"Well?"

"We're not from anywhere."

And so, on an early spring day, she heads off to school, the remnants of a father's brief foreign assignment in a Mac's Milk bag, her father left holding the remnants of a very Canadian experience: families that never kept track of themselves.

There are millions of us. People who can only listen while others speak of the precise date their United Empire Loyalist ancestors came north or their forefathers sailed from France.

People who have nothing to offer in return when others are able to name the exact ship or the very day the plane landed.

People who have nothing to match those who carry an extra language about with them or can point to heirlooms or oil portraits or, for that matter, a small bend in a northern river and say this is where they came from and who they are.

We can do none of this. We don't know how we got here, just that we are here. Perhaps no one wrote it down because, back then, no one could write. Perhaps some didn't want to remember. Who knows?

Who even thinks about it until a kid is running around a house looking for something – anything – she can take in for Heritage Day.

There are a great many such stories, but this one obviously, at some point, has someone from Scotland in it. And lots of Irish. No one knows when. And "why" does not even need to be asked. Farmers once, undoubtedly, they ended up so far back in the bush that, by the time this generation came around, no one even remembered how to plant.

On the mother's side there is, somewhere very far

back, a Welsh family sailing the Great Lakes. But the only memory with precise dates comes from another line, this time from England, this time sailing on a ship whose name was once written down and can still be found in a cardboard box on the Prairies.

Somewhere, sometime, they all began in the British Isles. Over time, there would be new links to France, Poland, Germany, Ukraine, Jamaica . . .

So by the time Heritage Day rolled around, she could mount a serious argument that she didn't come from anywhere.

The absurdity of this came home once before, months earlier, when an unsolicited letter arrived at the front door from Cousin Russell.

I call him "cousin," but the fact is neither I nor anyone else in this sprawling family has ever heard of a Russell MacGregor. Still, he wrote me from his office in Scarborough, Ontario, saying he had "exciting news for you and fellow MacGregors!"

Apparently, while the rest of us have been forgetting who we are, Russell has been involved in a major worldwide project that has led to the release of a major new book, *MacGregor Immigrants and Worldwide Descendants*, which is about to be published – presumably, as soon as I send Russell my $31.83.

"The first MacGregor found came to Montreal in 1825," Russell writes. "Her name was Margaret. . . . this First Edition is expected to be the only printing of the MacGregor book, ever. . . . You must order now!"

The reason, presumably, is that so many other books will be lined up for the presses, so many excited, desperate relatives have written back to Russell Mulroney, Russell Chretien, Russell McLaughlin, Russell Hnatyshyn, Russell Namagoose, Russell Singh, Russell Ng, and Russell Russell.

Perhaps if I'd only written earlier, she could have walked out of the house with *MacGregor Immigrants and Worldwide Descendants* under her arm instead of a Chinese peasant hat.

Or perhaps if only Canadians like us had a little more faith in who they are, she could have headed off to Heritage Day with a few family icons that would have told more about who we are and how we got here than a bagful of tourist trinkets from a place she has never been.

– A scrapbook of old, very tiny black-and-white photographs where everyone seems to be forever linking arms and skating on a frozen river.

– An axe that needs sharpening so badly it's gone rusty.

– An old hockey stick.

– A paddle.

– A piece of kindling.

– A coal-oil lamp.

And – to settle the argument once and for all about where she came from – her home address.

~

Even now, whenever I think of it I get cold feet. The feeling, however, is far too warm to cause shivers. It is a sensation so delicious that it is deliberately sought out each time four children who will never understand are force-marched through the Algonquin Park brush to stand on a strange point where each summer, a familiar point is made.

This, for their wearing father, is where it mattered most.

This is the "my time, my place" that Mordecai Richler found in Montreal's St. Urbain Street, that others have found in a paved-over back lane, along a certain river, on a farm that has passed into other hands and all too often into other use.

This particular place is on no tourist map of Algonquin Park, for it is nothing more than a point with a southern exposure on Lake of Two Rivers, a point that in 1988 contains several hemlock, a few cedar, some spruce, a lot of rocks – and a bit of hidden sawdust.

And the sawdust is what draws me back each summer.

If you kick where the blueberries now grow, and move a few stones where the ice house once stood, you will still find some, and if you take off your shoes and stand in this old sawdust and twist just so, the old feeling comes back: ice-cold sawdust that clogs in your toes and tickles your leg when it dries – wet, cold sawdust that was to children in other times what air-conditioning and slush cones are today.

And that is the nub of the problem. I want them to

stare and marvel. They want to pull in at the Lake of Two
Rivers store and see if they have slush cones.

I go to Algonquin Park and do not look for the
modern stores but where the Highland Inn once stood
on Cache Lake, and even though there is now a parking
lot on one side and a field of Queen Anne's lace on the
other, I can still trace out where the big log building held
ice blocks that were as thick in August as they had been
in February when the men with the long saws cut them
from the bay.

But always when I go to Algonquin Park, I go to the
point on Lake of Two Rivers where not so many years
ago the bulldozers came in and took away everything but
the memories.

It was here where my grandfather, Tom McCormick,
the chief ranger of Algonquin Park, began to build his
two-storey log house in 1939, and here where he signed
his name to the last piece of trim and wrote in the date:
Sept. 10, 1940.

When the bulldozers had finished, there was only a
broken board with his signature left lying on the ground.
That and his shaving mug, not even chipped, and a few
choice quartz stones from the fireplace he put together
with his own hands.

And down by where the ice house had stood by the
shore, a few shovelfuls of chilling sawdust.

It was here where the chief ranger lived, grew old with
Bea, and reluctantly retired when he was seventy. Here
where the children – some of whom, like my mother,

had been born in the Algonquin Park bush – came back with their own children for the long summers when the sky filled with sun and the ice house filled with lake trout as pink as the sky over Killarney Lodge when the sun finally set.

We came into the Park on the same day school let out, left the Park on the day before school let in. Two months and more of not knowing a single human being to whom you were not related.

Long after the old ranger had retired, he would still rise shortly after dawn, dress in ranger khakis, and begin a day so driven by ritual that it became the summer religion: the Union Jack up the flagpole, the shave at the kitchen table, the hour at the woodpile, another hour pumping water up from the lake for washing, the trip to the well for drinking water, the swim, and then, always, the walk.

The walks sometimes took place in the car – but they were always called walks, perhaps because it took so long just to get from the house to the old Dodge parked on the road – and they took in an Algonquin Park that few were privy to then and none are today.

At times he went to places well known and easily found. At the Canoe Lake docks he might touch upon the riddle of Tom Thomson's drowning, but never the far larger mystery of his life. The old ranger had known him well and liked him little. There was a family connection, but it was not to be mentioned.

There might be a snapping turtle to capture and drop

off at the Park museum or a visit to the Lands and Forests hangar on Smoke Lake. But more often than not it would be a hike in to an old logging camp along a path that existed only in his memory and from one old, overgrown blaze mark to the next, ever deeper into a bush that would deny direction.

Once there, he would root around the fallen boards for a leather hinge or a square nail and hold them out as if they contained some magical secret. Or else he would just sit, the forest silent but for the wheezing of an old man who could not leave it.

Every summer, he would take a huge sheet and head off for Spring Hill, and from there higher into the hills until, his khaki shirt black from sweating, he stood on the highest point of land in the entire park. And here he would unfurl the sheet into the wind, standing on the highest rock and pumping it like a flag for a solid hour, with nothing more than the hope that Bea would look down the lake and off into the hills, and maybe see that he had done exactly what he had set out to do, just to prove he could still do it.

Today, the trail he blazed up that hill is a nature lookout, and while there are signs to tell visitors the names of the trees and the lakes, there is nothing to tell of an old ranger who believed this to be the sweetest view a human eye can ever hope to hold – even if only for a single, exhausting hour once a summer.

There were long walks in search of moose, but they were rarely successful. Only thirty years ago, moose were rarity in Algonquin Park, but today are as common as the deer who would come every morning during the morning shave and wait for Bea to head out with a bowl of crusts.

No matter: a walk was considered a success if a whiskey jack was sighted or an antler found. If his face made contact with a fresh stream somewhere, it would leave behind a smile.

Not that it was all happy, for the forest is hardly as Thornton W. Burgess, author of all the *Tales of the Green Forest* books, described it.

The wolves howling from the far side of the lake made certain of that from the moment the old ranger put out the coal-oil lamp until the sleep that wouldn't come came anyway.

One morning, he had to go down to the nearest dump. The night before, a young girl, encouraged by her parents, had been feeding her cream soda to a small bear cub on the other side of the fence he had had the rangers erect. The girl pushed too close for a picture and the mother bear had hurried over and cuffed her back, an act not much appreciated by the girl's parents. They had complained, and now he was off to examine the outcome: seven black bears dead in a dump, each with a single gaping hole where the .30-.30 had ripped through the side or, since most were retreating in panic, the back.

That was one of the few days he ever called off the walk. An afternoon that might have been spent looking for fox holes was instead spent on the point listening to the sound of an axe on a whetstone, and the dreadful silence that followed stitched together with the persistence of his chopping.

The Park has changed since those days, more so than can be described. Even the dump is gone. The garbage is shipped out these days, often by air. And being a ranger is no longer a way of life, as it was then, an occupation like farming in that the work was never finished and an employee was never off. Today, the work of the old-style ranger is something they contract out, like the hiring of security guards. The old way is never going to return.

Today they talk of the battle between the loggers and those who call themselves "the users." Whatever that means. And whatever it does mean, it all seems so odd when remembering those who went before. Back so long ago, while the old ranger was shaving, his son-in-law, my father, would be headed out the long walk to the road, and fifteen minutes later he would be at work at the McRae Lumber Company on Whitefish Lake.

Two men who would be termed bitter enemies in another decade were then nothing of the kind. The logger would be furious if you stripped a birch tree for the paper; the ranger would never fail to say on one of his walks that this would never have been possible if it were not for the lumber companies thinning out the bush.

These are the kinds of things you think about on a summer day with your bare feet in old sawdust and your kids anxious to go. It is simply a point on a lake, a place where, while the old ranger was not buried there, he will live there forever.

For he knew what those who return again and again to this enchanted land come to understand: that such a park is not a highway nor a lodge nor a campground nor a government policy.

But a state of mind. A place where the fog plays along the morning water, where a campfire never grows low, where the loon laughs at another world that hopefully will never be let in by the east and west gates.

And where the sawdust is forever frozen.

~

At first, coming to Christmas dinner was just a short walk across the top of the hill, barely time for a nostril to lock. But later, once the second generation had moved out of the Valley to bring the third closer to schools and a few added opportunities they would come to regret, Christmas dinner began with an endless drive through the Park, the roads bare of other traffic and even sand, the only music – for the family was tone deaf and the radio out of all range – the sound of the tire chains dirging up Smoke Lake Hill and singing past the Opeongo turn.

It was the sounds that stayed with you. Not the first sight of smoke rising from the old people's winter home on the edge of the hill, not the first lick of heat that met you at the door, not the smell of turkey, the promise below the tree, not even the steam rising off the backs of the surly hogs in the pen at the foot of the hill.

No, it was what you heard: the chains that sang out each new arrival, the muffled pop of fast-moving doors, the rifle report of the party crackers, the laughter, the screaming that hurtled down off the toboggan hill and rose again as cheers from the cleared rink on the edge of the lake.

But above all, it was the voice of Santa Claus. He stood by — well, actually was suspended from — a wall in the kitchen, the blush long since faded from his cheeks and his tongue hanging halfway down to the floor.

It was in this tongue — a narrow, flexible red vinyl cord, unevenly serrated on the back — that the magic of Christmas resided, for every few minutes the old woman in charge of the dinner would back away from the wood stove, wipe her hands on her apron, push through the crowd of grandchildren gathered near the tip of the hanging tongue, and she would make Santa talk. Her thumbnail pressed tight to the serrated back of the cord, and her fingers wrapped loosely around the rest, the old woman would whip down the entire length of Santa's remarkable tongue, and for a moment the kitchen would be filled with his message: "Mer-ry Chrisss-mus, evvvree-buddeee."

Sometimes she would do it too fast and Santa would squeak slightly; sometimes too slow and he would growl.

But the old woman with the hard thumbnail was the one would could make him best understood.

When the grandchildren tried, what came out of Santa's mouth was the half-whistle a small hand makes when it rubs too quickly along something smooth. Santa at these times sounded more like the wind that was forming lassos of loose snow down toward the well.

But she could make him talk, and, for her, Christmas Day was a race between the demands of the woodstove and the calls of the small. It was, as anyone will tell you, another time, a time when there was simply no question about who belonged where on a Christmas Day.

The women belonged in the kitchen and around the large table where the meal would eventually be eaten. The children belonged outside on the ice or inside at the tip of Santa's tongue. And the men . . . well, it was another time, wasn't it?

The old man – a Park ranger who'd simply refused to retire – would have sawn enough planks and split enough kindling to heat the entire Upper Ottawa Valley, but there could never be enough.

While he, who prided himself on never having a drop of the demon in his house, sat in his rocker and teased whoever happened to be eyeing the skirt of the tree, the younger men took to the woodshed, where the gnaw of a Swede saw would soon eat into the laughter that followed each lie about the size of a certain lake trout or the number of partridge in a given shot line.

No one in the kitchen ever asked for wood, and when the men would file back in with thin loads and thick tongues, no one would bother pointing out that the bin was already filled and the turkey all but done. The call of the woodshed was simply part of the Christmas tradition.

In later years, long after the old ranger and his wife were gone and the house on the hill was no more, long after slabwood was a word no longer used and central heating had come to all, such gatherings would be marked by a crisis in the basement, a broken pump or a stubborn problem in the plumbing that would insist that the men of a certain age head down until the crisis had passed and the faces were as flushed as they'd ever turned in the woodshed.

In later years still, the problems would be with their own plumbing, but back then Christmas was, in part at least, a celebration of what can go conveniently wrong.

There was, back in the days when the ranger's house still stood on the hill, a certain five-year-old who had cried louder than the tire chains coming down off Smoke Lake Hill, the victim of Santa's shocking oversight, who had taken the cookies but neglected to leave behind the ordered drum.

It was a gloom that not even the old woman's hard nail on the back on Santa's tongue could lift. How dare he say "Merrry Chrissssmus, evreebuddeeee" when he himself had contrived to make it the most miserable gathering in history?

Too young for the woodshed, the boy could only mope around the box stove and wait for the sparks and the roar when the old ranger felt it time to improve the draw. The old man even let the youngster stoke at one point, but not even the chance to light a match under strict supervision could lift the disappointment over the missing drum.

Nor was the dinner much comfort, though the steam rose from the potatoes, a turkey drumstick was offered, and the old ranger made a great show of unfolding the crêpe hat from his party cracker and pulling it down over his eyes.

When it was over and the boy was sitting on the narrow steps leading up into the roughed-in sleeping room, the old ranger came to the foot of the stairs with a package that had not been under the tree. It had no bow, no name, nothing but scraps of wrapping paper barely hiding something that was certainly round and obviously tin. He motioned the sulking boy upstairs, ahead of him.

With the old ranger sitting on the edge of his bed in what was far more loft than second floor, the boy ripped open the paper but could not release the two wooden sticks that were heavily taped to the side of the drum. The old man brought out his jackknife, cut one free, and let the boy assist in cutting free the second.

"Stay up here," he said. "You won't be bothering anyone that way."

Later he brought up a coal-oil lamp and stayed long enough for a parade to pass, but then went back down to the sound of tea cups while the boy stayed behind to march again and again and again . . .

Eventually he tired enough to put down the sticks, and he lay in the bed with an arm around the drum, an eye on the shadows dancing against the far wall, and an ear to the pipes, listening while the delicious Valley mix of Irish and Scotch and German and Polish and French came riding up with the heat and told him that it was at least as warm down there as it was up here where the heat was rising.

And every once in a while, rising up through the far grating near the kitchen, there would come the quick march of sensible heels on linoleum, the cheers of whatever kids were still waiting, and the whisk of a hard thumbnail on serrated vinyl. And over the laughter and the growl of burning slabwood in twisting pipes, a remarkable voice would speak for the house that no longer stands on the edge of the hill.

"Merrrrr-yyy Chrisssmussss, evvereeebudddd-eeeeee . . ."

~

ONE OF THE advantages of being the only sportswriter to attend the annual Christmas Classic is that I can pretty well make of it what I want – including the score.

This year was more special than usual. Under the circumstances – no baseball, no hockey, the state of the CFL – the Christmas Classic had become, by default, the sporting event of the season.

But did the Christmas Classic take advantage of its fans? Not for one moment. It cost nothing to get in and nothing to park. Only two picked up souvenirs – one an ankle that turned the wrong way, the other an accidental slash across the shin – and the concession stand was, as usual, a long walk back down the road, free beer and Diet Coke cooling on the back porch.

Mind you, there have never been any fans to take advantage of: everyone who comes to the Christmas Classic plays. Rule No. 1.

Perhaps some of you need a little explanation. More likely, some of you have played your own Christmas Classics and are still glowing in that necessary reminder that somewhere, at the core of the games we came to worship, the reason for playing was fun.

The Christmas Classic I am reporting on takes place each December 25, at noon, on a country back road a good four hours from Ottawa. If you saw it on a map, you'd say you had never been there. If you saw it being played, you'd know you've always been there.

This year, there were a solid dozen players, men and

women, ages twelve to nearly sixty, all related. Sometimes there are more, sometimes less. The stars of the earliest Classics now tend to play nets and lean on their sticks; the stars of this year's game weren't even born when the first ones were played.

There is no record of the scores, but an annual record by photograph: players growing, hairlines receding, shoulders widening, bellies sagging.

If they kept a shot clock at matches like this, they would have to distinguish between verbal shots and shots on goal. And everyone knows which ones count for more.

This year will be remembered for the lack of snow and the way those in goal whined about getting sand in their face every time someone took a shot. Other years have had their own special note: the year the cars froze, the year of the blizzard, the year it rained, the year they broke the gender barrier, the year the youngest lost a boot, the last year a loved cousin could play.

Sometimes we wonder how it came to take on such significance. It began a generation ago by accident, but now stands with tree and turkey as a symbol of the season.

There is nothing fancy about it. A cousin who plays tennis supplies the balls. An oldtimer who shoots right and another who shoots left (me) bring extra sticks. We chipped in several years ago for two Canadian Tire nets – not to be fancy, but because the older ones playing goal were getting sick of chasing balls down the road.

You want a score? One side won, one side lost; then we switched sides.

We play, as so many others do this time of year, because it is the only time we are all together.

And because, many years ago, some of the older ones realized that, in the end, memory is the most-lasting gift of all.

EPILOGUE

The Road Home

Back in the Fifties, when everyone lived forever and there were no problems in the world, our father would play a trick that makes me shudder far more today than it ever did then. He had bought the only new car he would ever own – a 1956 Pontiac, which we could ill-afford and about which, clearly, there had been no consultation with our mother – and he would pile us into it and head through Algonquin Park to pick up groceries at Whitney or visit one of the dozens, seemingly thousands, of relatives who lived in that area of the Ottawa Valley known as the Upper Madawaska.

If he came up behind a logging truck heading out from the mill he worked at, or a carload of what we ridiculed as gawking tourists – people who would actually *stop* for a deer or a moose standing along the side of the road – he would often wait until the worst possible moment to pass. Ideal, to him, was a short, steep hill where the two white lines running up the middle of the road clearly warned against passing, and he would pull out and around and suddenly start yelping like a scared puppy as he pumped the gas pedal and made the big car jump and hop as though it would never, ever, make it, finally flooring the pedal at what seemed like the last possible moment so we would roar past the other vehicle, over the hill, and safely away.

There is much that could be read into this behaviour. Our father could indeed be silly and irresponsible, often both at the same time, and often with a glorious joy that still stays with us. Perhaps he needed the thrill of living on the edge, if only for a moment. Perhaps he knew, as someone who lived and worked most of his life in the Park, that the chances of another car coming the other way at any given time were remote indeed. Still, he should have known better.

A dozen times or more a year, we drive that same road. I rarely go over one particular hill nearing Brewer Lake without thinking of him pulling out when he shouldn't have – something I would never do, and not just because the traffic is steady – and, I must admit, I smile to myself despite the urging of common sense. I miss us all in that car, even if the one driving is taking a stupid chance and the one beside him is shaking her head in disgust. We in the backseat are together, and laughing, and the shared memory has a value of its own, ever more precious to those who are left to carry it on.

When I switched over to covering sports, I essentially stopped writing about the four who sometimes ride in our own backseat. In part it was because time didn't allow. In part it was because the children were racing headlong into ages that didn't lend themselves to public scrutiny. There are funny columns to be written about smoking and tattoos and nose-rings and boyfriends and girlfriends and alternative music, but they wouldn't be funny to everyone: much like a foreign correspondent, a family columnist has far more freedom when his subjects do not read what has been written.

They are growing up, just as I had to grow up. Soon after the Fifties had passed, I came to understand, much to my everlasting regret, that people did not live forever and the world was hardly a perfect place. Neither did it make you a better and wiser person merely because you were used to seeing deer and moose by the side of the road and did not stop. The first time we went to those cities from which the tourists we ridiculed came, the roles were reversed. They may have been frightened of the bears that gathered by the Lake of Two Rivers dump; but my older brother, Jim, and I were scared to go to the bathroom in Maple Leaf Gardens, where the stainless steel urinals stretched as long as a log boom.

A dozen times or more a year, we pile into the car to go back this same road, driving from Ottawa to Huntsville through Algonquin Park for Christmas and Easter, and in summer for the lake, and in the fall and spring when we can. There are still grandparents and houses to visit, though in the last year we have lost one of each, the grandparent the one who used to pull out to pass when he shouldn't. The car he finally met coming head-on the other way turned out to be pneumonia, and the last laugh with which he left the world was to tell the nurse he didn't think he'd need a shave in the morning – but I don't know how you'd write a funny column about dying. Even when the subject under discussion is eighty-eight and couldn't possibly have asked for anything more out of life – with the possible exception of a Stanley Cup in Detroit.

When we head "home," we head up Highway 17 toward Renfrew. We drive along the west side of the Ottawa River, where Champlain once believed he was paddling "to the Kingdom of China and the East Indies," and where, a few years ago, a religious group built a gift-shop in a replica of Noah's Ark and opened up a water slide to get the tourists to stop. We never stop. Unlike Champlain and the Ark builders, we know where we are and where we're going.

Five times on this trip we cross the Madawaska River. Once at Arnprior, once at Madawaska, once at Whitney, once over a small branch at Lake of Two Rivers, and once just before the Madawaska has its beginning in the Park at a lake appropriately named Source. For reasons that escape even me, I tend to repeat the same story at some point during these symbolic crossings: the children should know that their father was born on the banks of the Madawaska where it passes through the village of Whitney, that he summered on the Madawaska where it widens to Lake of Two Rivers and now lives where the Madawaska flows with the Ottawa down toward the St. Lawrence. The Madawaska, therefore, is a constant in our family. The children could care less. Also a constant is the dog. And loud music.

We pass through the exquisite little town of Eganville, where my father was born in 1907 and where my mother moved from Algonquin Park in order to attend high school. Here – excelling in baseball and hockey – he gained a love of sports that lasted his whole life. After he had reached an age where every friend he had ever had, as well as two sisters and three brothers, were all dead, he summed up the meaning of sports to him in a single comment. "It gives me something to look forward to," he said. The morning papers held the box scores and game summaries. He had to know, and he had to get up if he was going to find out.

We drive through Golden Lake, past the reserve and through Deacon, and by the Tramore Road, down which our great-aunt Minnie once lived in what seemed another century. Her wake is one of my earliest memories, most assuredly the sharpest, and even today there is a small part of my brain that swirls with images of a plain casket in the drawing room, keeners wailing, the women in the sitting room with tea, and the men in the woodshed with a liquid much the same colour, but straight out of small bottles they kept in the inside pocket of ill-fitting jackets. The men later carried the casket on their shoulders up the road to the little cemetery, used rough rope to lower her into the ground, and then took turns throwing down spadesful of stone-peppered earth.

The connection here seems more remote than it should be. All over this country there are small pockets like the Ottawa Valley – another Madawaska in New Brunswick, Cape Breton, Newfoundland, Northern Quebec and Ontario, prairie towns, the territories – where the change between generations stretches more than seems reasonable or possible. When we pass through Whitney, I always point up the dirt road that heads into Airy, where not so long ago my mother, Helen, cared for three in diapers and had no electricity and no running water, with the well a good quarter-mile away, most of it downhill. I know of no stronger person on earth. She had been born in Algonquin Park – the daughter of a ranger and a tiny woman so tough I once saw her chase a black bear out of her garden with nothing more than a raised frying pan.

I point and I talk, but no one hears. They have their Walkmans on, and those who do not have taken control of the tape deck, and the Smashing Pumpkins are screaming "*The killer in me is the killer in you!*" and it is all beyond explaining anyway. They come from a modern city home with two bathrooms and a sink in the laundry room, and still it is never enough. Their grandmother had no tap, no pump, and an outdoor toilet, and would eventually raise four children with a husband who spent six days a week in the bush. She didn't even have a radio for company.

I babble on through the Park, the kids raising their eyes from comics and books and tape players long enough to acknowledge a moose or a deer, but we never actually stop for them. We do stop, at least once a summer, at the point at Lake of Two Rivers where the Park ranger and his wife built their magnificent two-storey log home and where we spent every summer until the old ranger died and circumstances forced the sale to an American couple who eventually tore it down and moved it, log by numbered log, out of the Park.

This is a place so familiar, I am instantly lost when I reach it. There, the fireplace crumbles. There, the footings can still be found. There, the ice house once stood. There, the summer kitchen, the sleeping cabins, the picnic table, the garden in which my grandmother once scared the wits out of a huge black bear.

Some of the places are harder to find each year. The miniature village my sister, Ann, made of tiny stones and moss is lost in the pine growth. If I push in under the scratchy lower branches and kick at the rust-coloured needles, a small stone might roll, and hope and faith will call it a step or a cornerstone of that magical world she created that long-ago summer. With the children's help last year, we uncovered a handful of these precious stones to bury with her – cancer the vehicle coming head-on the other way. "That," she said at one point, as her brothers sat by her bedside, reminiscing about this spot in Algonquin Park, "is what matters most." And now it matters even more.

The kids have invented their own ritual here. We come and we change into our bathing suits and we dive from the high rocks, out into the water that runs from Source Lake down through Whitney and on into the Ottawa River. When they dive I can see Ann's elegant style in the one who became a competitive diver. They use the same toe- and handholds we used to climb out and dive back in. They bring their friends, and we all swim out to a place we called "the duck rock" and hold hands and all sink down together to see how deep we can go. We shout and try to make out what people are saying. The words don't matter. The shouting does. It says we are still here.